MASTERWORKS OF WORLD DRAMA

ROME
AND
THE MIDDLE AGES

Anthony Caputi

CORNELL UNIVERSITY

D. C. HEATH AND COMPANY

Acknowledgments

THE MIRACLE OF THE BLIND MAN AND THE CRIPPLE by
Andrieu de la Vigne. From *Representative Medieval and Tudor Plays,*
translated and edited by Henry W. Wells and Roger S. Loomis.
Copyright 1942 Sheed & Ward Inc., New York.

THE MYSTERY OF ADAM, anon. Translated by Edward Noble
Stone, by permission of the University of Washington Press.

THE TRIAL OF JOSEPH AND MARY, anon. Modernized version
by Barry Adams.

*The drawings on pages 48 and 106 are
by* PETER KAHN, *Cornell University.*

Library of Congress Catalog Card number 68-15400

CONTENTS

Pageant wagon with a performance of a late-medieval mystery play
at Coventry. After a reconstruction by Thomas Sharp, 1825.
Photo Radio Times Hulton Picture Library

vi   THE DRAMA OF ROME AND THE MIDDLE AGES

THE DRAMA OF *Rome and the Middle Ages*

THE EMERGENCE OF ROMAN DRAMA There is a popular old story which tells of certain players from Etruria, an area in Italy rich in early dramatic activity, who were summoned to Rome during a plague in 364 B.C. to placate the gods with their primitive musical entertainments. If the story can be credited, it gives us early evidence of two important circumstances in the history of Roman drama: that it was closely associated with religion and that it had developed native forms at quite an early date.

The story of Roman drama before Plautus and Terence, in fact, is largely an account of a number of such musical entertainments and crude farces which had developed at different times in different parts of the Italian peninsula and Sicily. In Etruria there were the ancient Fescennine Verses, so-called perhaps after the town of Fesiennium in South Etruria, or perhaps for their association with the *fascinum,* a word which often meant phallus. Originally associated with harvest festivals and later with weddings and triumphs, these entertainments were exuberant, impromptu revelries consisting chiefly of crude jests. Gradually, they were combined with Etruscan dances and performed to the accompaniment of a flute, and in this mixed form, comprising singing, dancing, and speeches, though still "plotless" in structure, they became known as the *saturae* or "medleys." It was probably *saturae* which the Etruscan players presented in Rome in 364 B.C.

Meanwhile, in Southern Italy and Sicily at least two simple farce forms developed early. The mime, of uncertain origin but probably borrowed from Greece, was both the oldest and the most durable of the early dramatic types. It consisted of ribald scenes of low life, frequently stories of adultery, presented with song, dance, dialogue, and harlequinade. By the time of Plautus—late in the third century—strolling companies of mime performers are known to have circulated throughout Italy and to have included women among them to enhance the opportunities for the obscenity for which the form was famous. The *phylax* farces, on the other hand, trace directly to Greek sources in that the actors wore Old Comedy costumes and the action consisted of outlandish burlesques of legend.

The numerous *phylax* vase paintings, which give remarkably rich evidence of these crude little playlets, vividly show the wild extravagance of these dramatizations of Zeus's amours and the gods' absurdities.

Apparently, the first native form to involve a connected series of events, or plot, was the farce known as the *Fabula Atellana* (so named from its development in Campania and association with the town of Atella). The *Atellanae* presented simple stories drawn from country or village life, and for a time they and their masked performers were extremely popular, though they probably did not influence drama elsewhere in Italy until the end of the third century B.C., when they were brought to Rome with great acclaim. Thereafter the form was gradually assimilated by the mime until it survived in its own right only in the literary exercises of litterateurs, but it has the curious, if problematical, distinction of perhaps having exerted a long-range influence on later comedy by way of four comic characters of inexhaustible possibilities: Pappus, the good-humored, gullible old man; Bucco, the fool; Maccus, the stupid, gluttonous oaf; and Dossenus, the sharp-tongued, witty hunchback.

As the *Atellanae* yielded to the mime, one other important native form, the pantomime, emerged. The pantomime was largely, but not entirely, a drama without dialogue and was performed by one or more dancers while a chorus sang the story. In its fully developed form it was staged with lavish scenery, costumes, and music; and in its heyday it enjoyed both immense popularity and the praise of a great many serious writers who otherwise would have nothing to do with the theater. With the mime, the pantomime survived into the period of the decadence, gradually succumbing with most other surviving forms to the degrading influences of obscenity and cheap excitement.

Against this mixed background of popular forms Roman drama took its first decisive steps toward the achievement of Plautus and Terence with the work of Livius Andronicus (*c.*284–204 B.C.), a manumitted Greek slave from Tarentum, a city in Magna Graecia well-known for its interest in the theater. Andronicus, an actor and an early translator of the *Odyssey,* is believed to have provided the first translation of a Greek comedy and tragedy for a festival celebrating the end of the first Punic War in 240 B.C.; in all, the titles of some nine tragedies and three comedies which he translated from the Greek still exist. Although he was a colorless and ungraceful writer, Andronicus is important because he introduced Graeco-Roman tragedy and the *Fabula Palliata* into the Roman tradition. Thereafter, Rome's closest approaches to dramatic excellence were to be found in the adaptations made by Roman writers of Greek tragedies and comedies, particularly in the *Palliatae,* the Romanized versions of Greek New Comedies. The beginning made by Andronicus, fortunately, was quickly taken up by writers of greater talent.

When Andronicus was presenting his first plays, Gnaeus Naevius (*c.*260–*c.*100 B.C.), the first Roman dramatist of note, was already a young man. During something more than a thirty year period Naevius produced at least forty plays, of which the titles of thirty-four *Palliatae* and seven Graeco-Roman tragedies are recorded. In addition, he created the native tragic form known as the *Fabula Praetexta,* in which he drew his subjects from Roman legend and history and pointed the way toward the later comic form known as the *Fabula Togata* by using incidents from Italian life in a number of plays, including his most famous, the *Tarentilla*. Of all this work only fragments remain, but enough to indicate that Naevius wrote with dignity and power. From Terence we learn that the important practice of *contaminatio,* by which Roman playwrights combined the plots or parts of plots of two or more Greek originals in constructing a *Palliata,* was already evident in Naevius' work.

Younger than Naevius, indeed even younger than Plautus, was Quintus Ennius (260–*c.*170 B.C.), a half-Greek, half-Italian from Southern Italy who is now generally considered the first great Roman poet. Ennius was the last Roman playwright to write both tragedies and comedies: we have the titles of two *Palliatae,* two *Praetextae,* and about twenty Graeco-Roman tragedies. He must have been especially fond of Euripides, because he based about half of these tragedies on Euripidean originals, which, as the fragments suggest, he usually heightened for rhetorical effect. A greater poet than a playwright, however, Ennius was remembered by later ages chiefly for his epic poetry.

THE AGE OF PLAUTUS AND TERENCE With the work of Naevius and Ennius we enter the period of Plautus and Terence and of that brief, rather incomplete flowering of drama in ancient Italy that constituted Rome's legacy to the drama of the west. This period runs from about 225 B.C. to about 160 B.C., and, like all times of important dramatic activity, it witnessed a peculiar confluence of development in play production, as well as in play-writing.

Although the earlier association of dramatic entertainment with religion had little meaning by this time, the practice of producing plays at religious festivals persisted; indeed the theaters were still built near the temple of the god being honored. In Rome, however, festivals were conspicuously times for merry-making and theaters quite simply places for entertainment, and unlike the situation in Greece, festivals in Italy were quite numerous, in fact toward the end of the Republic and under the Empire festivals so numerous as to be commonplace. Perhaps the most important of them was that known as the *Ludi Romani,* a festival associated with the cult of Jupiter Capitolinus and celebrated in September. Originally—probably in the sixth century B.C.—it took place on one day, though gradually it grew until under Augustus it covered fifteen. As a festival, it included parades, chariot races, beast fights, wrestling, boxing, rope dancing, and, apparently during the first few days, plays; and like the Dionysiac celebrations in Greece, it was held under the supervision of the Senate, which defrayed all expenses, though it did not sponsor dramatic contests.

The arrangements for public productions were usually handled by the Magistrate in charge of the festival, who contracted for the plays with the professional manager, or *dominus,* of an acting company. The *dominus,* usually a freedman and an actor himself, apparently bought plays outright from a playwright and then, once commissioned, took entire charge of the production. The whole operation was strictly a matter of business: the playwright wrote for money and the *dominus* produced for it; and, typically, the *dominus* ran his acting troupe with an iron hand. Since actors, known as *histriones,* were usually slaves, they were relatively abundant and were acquired in sufficient numbers so that there was no need for doubling in parts. They were trained for tragedy, comedy, mime, or pantomime and flogged when they did not achieve an acceptable standard of performance. Unlike their Greek counterparts, they had virtually no civic privileges and few, if any, fringe benefits. Although their social position was somewhat improved later by the great actor Roscius (*fl.*50 B.C.), who became the intimate of many men in high positions, they were unmistakably disreputable. For the most part these players were trained in a declamatory mode of acting, as well as in singing and dancing. The best of them were praised for clarity of utterance and gracefulness and appropriateness of gesture which suggests a distinctively rhetorical, formalized style of playing.

The physical theater in the age of Plautus and Terence was a temporary structure erected for a single run of plays and torn down afterwards. Profoundly influenced by Greek precedents at all stages of its development, in this, its earliest period, it was notably simple. To begin with, Roman theaters were usually built on flat ground with the result that the *cavea,* or viewing place, was much slower to develop than the *theatron* had been in Greece. Through most of Plautus' career, seats were unknown unless the spectators brought them themselves. The physical structure consisted simply of a scene-building with a long, low wooden platform at its front and wooden walls at the back and flanking both ends. In the earliest scene-buildings these back walls were blank, though they contained three usable doors (there were two more at the sides), but in time they were painted and ornamented with columns, niches, arches, and statuary. In front of the scene-building was the orchestra, an open semicircular space that was not so often used as a playing area as it was reserved for dignitaries, and around the *orchestra,* though last in developing, was the *cavea,* or semicircular viewing place, where in Plautus' time spectators usually stood. In time these buildings, though temporary, became lavish in their appointments; yet we hear that even after the construction of the first stone scene-building in 174 B.C., spectators still had to bring their own seats.

Our chief source of information about these theaters are the permanent stone theaters which were built later and some of which are still standing. Pompey's theater, which seated 40,000 spectators, was completed in 55 B.C. and was followed in 13 B.C. by the theater of Marcellus; thereafter smaller theaters were built all over the Roman world. Ironically, these sumptuous monuments served for the most trivial dramatic fare, even as they established an architectural model that was profoundly to influence theater buildings of later periods. In them we find the conventional three-part Greek structure as one architectural unit combining the scene-building, the *orchestra,* and the *cavea.* The *cavea,* by this time a semicircular gallery of stone seats adjoined to the scene-building at either end of its semicircle, rested on an impressive foundation with underground passageways like those of our modern football stadiums. The scene-building became with the change to stone even more intricate in design and more ornate than it had been in wood, and along the front edge of its stage a richly embroidered curtain was hung which was dropped into a trough at the beginning of the play and raised at the end.

The principal playing area in this theater, as well as in the earlier wooden one, was the long, low platform of the scene-building, and its use was governed by fairly strict conventions. The platform was always understood to be a street, while the doors in the back wall were the doors of neighboring houses in comedy and of a palace in tragedy. The exit to the actors' left was understood to lead to the Forum, while the one to their right led to the harbor. Even the scene-paintings with which the front of the scene-building was decorated to assist in establishing locale were regularly supported by three standard *periaktoi,* the triangular columns introduced in Greece, one for each of the standard scenes, the tragic, the comic, and the satyric. Oddly enough, the most variable part of the physical stage was the altar placed in various locations on it. Sometimes it served as a place for worship, sometimes as a sanctuary for comic characters trying to escape a beating.

Like the stage, the details of production reflected a mixture of native and Greek tendencies. In matters of dress the actors followed the later Greeks: tragic actors wore long gowns and high boots, or buskins, comic actors short gowns and sandals. In the earliest period masks were apparently not used, except in the *Atellanae* and the *Phylax* farces, but by the time of Plautus and Terence they too were coming into use, and by the end of the second century they were always worn, except in the mimes. In other respects, however, the Romans did not follow the Greeks as much as they did their own incurable penchant for spectacular realism. The chorus was never prominent in Roman drama. In tragedy it was sometimes used for interludes; in comedies it seems not to have been used at all. Instead, by the first century B.C. the producers were filling out tragic spectacles with real executions, real combats, and crowd scenes involving hundreds of captives, horses, and chariots. It is recorded that on the occasion of the opening of Pompey's theater in 55 B.C., 600 mules were used in a production of Accius' *Clytemnestra.*

Our heritage in Roman drama, however, traces neither to the stone theaters (except architecturally) nor to the sumptuous spectacles produced in them, but almost entirely to the comedies written by Plautus and Terence for the temporary wooden theaters of the first quarter of the second century. After several vigorous careers, Titus Maccius Plautus (*c.*254–184 B.C.) turned his prodigious talents to play-writing in about 210 B.C. and, in the brief time remaining to him, wrote probably some 48 plays. Of this work, the twenty-one which are extant constitute our principal examples of the *Fabula Palliata* in its perfected form. In general, Plautus' adaptations of Greek New Comedies were more boisterous and exuberant than their originals, and in them he gave greater prominence to women and to love—probably because women in Roman society enjoyed more freedom than Greek women—and to musical elements. Yet certainly Plautus was no mere translator or hack adapter. Despite the importance of his debt to Menander, among others, he invariably qualified his borrowed materials with abundant local color in the form of Roman customs, legal procedures, manners, and place-names, and in re-shaping his sources he regularly combined plays and omitted or drastically altered scenes or parts of them, if such changes made for greater liveliness. It was chiefly as a stylist, however, that Plautus imposed on his Greek originals the hilarity and raucousness that typify his work. As a master of racy, high-spirited dialogue, a gifted jokester and punster, and a consummate metrist, he was most a creator and least an imitator in conferring on his plays, by way of their language, the pungency and coarse ebullience peculiarly his own.

Younger than Plautus, Publius Terentius Afer, called Terence (185–c.159 B.C.), was more patrician and sophisticated than his great contemporary. Terence apparently came as a slave from Carthage to Rome, where as a young man he was freed and taken up by the aristocratic Scipio and his circle. Between 166 and 160 B.C. he produced six *Palliatae,* all of them like the work of his predecessors, but all more carefully wrought as dramatic structures, more delicate in sentiment, and more polished and refined in style. Julius Caesar once said of Terence that he was deficient in comic spirit. However true this claim may have been, Terence clearly scorned popular taste by preferring quiet comic effects to boisterous mirth and by contriving plots that demanded more attention from his audiences than a typical Plautine action. Among his many technical achievements, he introduced the structural conception of a double action, or double plot, extended and complicated the use of surprise, gave greater attention to characterization, and set standards in verbal style by taking great pains to achieve elegance and correctness.

Taken together, the plays of Plautus and Terence constitute the principal tradition of classical comedy; they provided immensely influential models for later comic playwrights, particularly after Alexandrian editors had imposed the five-act structure on them.

Unfortunately, the story of tragedy in this period of flowering is rather less illustrious than that of comedy and is preserved only in fragments of plays. After Ennius, Marcus Parcuvius (c.220–130 B.C.) was considered the chief Roman tragedian for many decades. He was a painter and poet as well as a playwright who, as a learned writer, followed his Greek models closely and favored complicated plots; of his work we have fragments of twelve Graeco-Roman tragedies and one *Praetexta.* Lucius Accius (170–c.85 B.C.) was the last tragic dramatist of consequence. He wrote in a flamboyant and spirited, if rather rhetorical, style both Graeco-Roman tragedies and *Praetextae,* of which the titles and fragments of some fifty Graeco-Roman tragedies and of two *Praetextae* still exist. After Accius few, if any, new tragedies were written, and no writers followed the writing of tragedies for the theater as a profession.

THE DECLINE OF ROMAN DRAMA   Under the late Republic and the Empire a deterioration became evident in all the dramatic forms (except mime and pantomime) as each either fell into disuse or became primarily a literary exercise. Old tragedies continued to be produced for a time and even enjoyed a brief revival because of the impulse provided by the great actor Aesopus (*fl.*70 B.C.); but the interest did not last. Steadily and decisively all practical connection between tragedy as a dramatic form and as a theatrical performance disappeared, until finally the only activity in the genre came from literary dilettantes who occasionally wrote Graeco-Roman closet tragedies never intended for production. The *Fabula Praetexta,* likewise, was all but ignored until the first century A.D. when it too underwent a brief revival as a literary form. Strangely enough, it was this revival that produced our only complete extant example of the type in the anonymous *Octavia.*

The decline in comedy, meanwhile, was not so rapid, but was no less real. After Terence a number of writers continued for a time to produce *Palliatae;*

then gradually it yielded to a new native form known as the *Fabula Togata,* which presented actions based on the life of the Roman and Italian middle classes and which, in turn, after a brief period of popularity, became exclusively a literary form. Finally, even the hardy *Atellanae* became a favorite form for literary exercise in the first century B.C., after which, although it held on in the theater as an after-piece until the first century A.D., it too died out.

The only dramatist of consequence to emerge from this general picture of flagging interest and diminished energy was Lucius Annaeus Seneca, called Seneca the Younger (*c.*4 B.C.–65 A.D.). As the son of an eminent Roman family and the intimate of emperors, Seneca had aristocratic literary tastes, but no real connection with the theater. Best known for his philosophical and moral essays, he nonetheless wrote nine tragedies based on plays by Aeschylus, Sophocles, and Euripides, which, unlike their models, were designed for reading or at most for a recitation of the sort that was increasingly popular in his time. Seneca's great importance rests on the fact that, though he was scarcely conscious of himself as a dramatist and had no influence on what remained of the history of Roman drama, his modifications in Graeco-Roman tragedy produced a model of tragic structure that was to have a profound influence in the Renaissance, when the humanists were to look to his work for their examples of classical tragedy. With their emphasis on violence, sensationalism, moral declamation, and supernatural elements, Seneca's "blood and thunder" tragedies provided a repository of structural devices and conventions of unrivalled value to later tragic dramatists.

The decline of the drama in Rome is chiefly to be traced, then, through the deterioration of the dramatic forms, particularly Graeco-Roman tragedy and the *Fabula Palliata,* forms in which high literary and dramatic standards had been achieved. As with so much else, of course, the underlying causes of the theatrical decline are buried in the story of Rome's decline and fall. With the end of the Republic and the establishment of the Empire, Rome gained staggering wealth and power, but also lost many things, including a taste for drama of merit. Although the number of holidays, religious or otherwise, during which plays could be produced was gradually increased until under the Empire in 354 A.D. there were 101 holidays each year, the Roman populace preferred to see circuses and gladiatorial combats. Indeed, when the great stone theaters that constitute one of Rome's most important legacies to western drama were being built in the last half of the first century B.C., the old tragedies and comedies produced in them were already yielding to more trivial and degrading fare; before long these magnificent structures housed nothing more important than mimes, panto-mimes, recitations, and even gladiatorial combats.

The only dramatic forms to survive into the Christian era, in fact, were the mimes and pantomimes, and they persisted by increasingly emphasizing licentious-ness. Yet with the growth of the Christian Church, even these forms finally found their antagonists. Outraged by the depravity of these performances, the Church first criticized and attempted restraints, then, when the mime performers responded by ridiculing church officialdom and church services, excommunicated the players. In the sixth century A.D. the Emperor Justinian closed the theaters altogether. The last notice of a performance in Rome occurs in a letter from 534 A.D.

THE DEVELOPMENT OF CHRISTIAN LITURGI-
CAL DRAMA

What have been popularly called the Dark Ages were truly dark for the theater: dramatic activity as we understand it virtually disappeared for centuries. The mime performers dispersed over southern Europe to become part of the minstrelsy in company with acrobats, animal trainers, jugglers, singers, and story tellers. Known by different names in different places, they performed at fairs, in taverns, and in noble houses, singing, dancing, telling stories of knights and ladies, and carrying the news of the day. Some of them specialized in certain early dramatic forms like monologues or dialogues, and some probably performed simple little plays, though there is very little precise information about such activity. Although in these ways they undoubtedly kept certain features of the classical legacy alive, it is doubtful that they exerted more than a feeble and indirect influence on the drama to be born after centuries of silence.

Classical drama, insofar as it was known at all, was chiefly kept alive by learned members of monastic communities. From the tenth century we have an anonymous *Passion of Christ* in Latin which incorporates several hundred lines from Euripides, and the work of Hrosvitha, a nun from the Benedictine Abbey at Gandersheim, Saxony. Hrosvitha provided the exception to the general theatrical silence by writing six comedies in Latin modelled on Terence's style in which she glorified chastity and martyrdom. The plays are relatively undistinguished and their influence was negligible; but we are reasonably certain that they were performed and what we imagine to have been their circulation throughout the Benedictine community implies both a knowledge of classical drama and an interest that probably affected, if only indirectly, the first efforts made by Benedictine clerics to write religious playlets.

Perhaps the chief keepers of the flame of theater during this long period of relative inactivity, however, were neither the minstrels nor the clerics, but the common folk who in all parts of Europe continued to celebrate seasonal changes with primitive dramatic ceremonies remarkably similar to those performed earlier in Greece. Again the evidence of the long evolution from ritual to simple drama is incomplete, but it is sufficient to indicate clear lines of development from carnival ceremonies, May Day games, and New Year's festivities to rudimentary farces and folk plays of various kinds. In Italy and France the comic characters and situations which were developed from the Carnival festivities became the background material for village square farces and simple comedies offered by small troupes of professional players. Everywhere the pattern by which the old year is killed and the new year is born is retained in quasi-epic dramatizations of a combat in which the protagonist first dies and then is resurrected. In the English Mummers' Play, for example, the protagonist, usually Saint George, is invariably killed by his antagonist, usually a Turk with a black face, and then in a final episode revived by a comic doctor. Folk drama of this kind was an important and rich part of medieval culture; yet despite its links with religion and seasonal rites it would be misleading to say that it, any more than other dramatic survivals during the so-called Dark Ages, made an important contribution to the central dramatic achievement of the Middle Ages.

For all practical purposes the drama born of the medieval church began from scratch and profited from the example of antiquity and from contemporary dramatic activities only after it was well under way. It all began with the musical embellishments that gradually crept into the choral portions of the Mass. Although, theoretically, no departure from the text of the missal was permitted in the celebration of the Mass, gradually additions were made, particularly to the choir's part, and particularly for the special Masses of great religious feasts. These embellishments are known as musical tropes, and they consist of the elaborate variations by which single syllables are prolonged. When these embellishments reached a stage of great complexity, a problem of memorization developed for the choirs, and to aid the choir members, words were gradually associated with the separate notes, words which probably had some relevance to the religious holiday being celebrated. By a very slow and mysterious process these sung passages came to have a dramatic content; they are known as dramatic tropes.

The earliest dramatic trope of which we know anything is the *Quem Quaeritis* ("Whom are you seeking?"), an Easter trope dealing with the coming of the three Marys to Christ's tomb on Easter morning. In his *Regularis Concordia* (963–975 A.D.) Saint Ethelwold describes the model for use in Benedictine abbeys in England and outlines a simple playlet in which one priest holding a palm leaf is seated at a tomb in the church and is approached by three other priests carrying censers while the choir sings the story. But far more important is the text preserved at the Abbey in St. Gall, Switzerland and dating from the beginning of the tenth century: here we have eighteen lines of dialogue consisting of the opening question, "Whom are you seeking?" and the brief conversation that follows. In certain later versions of still other texts some visual detail is preserved: in one the burial clothes were examined and at the conclusion a procession singing the glory of the resurrection was formed.

This early example of the Easter play presents clear evidence of the way the liturgical drama emerged from the tropes. Through most of their history these playlets were composed in Latin and chanted and acted by members of the clergy. Little attempt was made to render the episodes realistically. Some part of the church interior was used for the "stage"—perhaps one of the tombs in the church for the *Quem Quaeritis*—and only the simplest properties were introduced. Gradually, however, even the briefest episodes were elaborated on, and more and more material was dramatized until playlets had been developed to embrace much of the Christmas and Ascension services, as well as the Easter service. With this elaboration the entire church interior was pressed into use: we hear of platforms placed against the pillars up and down the nave and of a scenic arrangement by which the entrance to the crypt became the mouth of Hell; we can imagine, further, that a great many of the members of the religious community were required temporarily to become actors. Yet, however complex the productions became, their purpose remained essentially that so clear in the *Quem Quaeritis:* to represent God's greatness and goodness in reenactments of Bible story and to generate in the beholder a sense of the infinite wonder and beneficence of God's works.

By the late thirteenth and early fourteenth centuries almost all of the New and much of the Old Testament had been dramatized, as well as much material from saints' lives. The playwrights were certainly clerics, though practically nothing is known of them beyond a few names like Geoffrey of Gorham and

Hilarius. The plays continued to be performed inside the churches, or at least in religious communities, but, gradually, the vernacular insinuated itself into the otherwise learned texts: *The Mystery of Adam* from the twelfth century is largely in French;/a Shrewsbury manuscript preserves parts of three plays that were, apparently, mostly in English; and the elaborate text for the Montecassino *Passion* has choruses in Italian. In the period of liturgical drama's fullest development, moreover, lay-performers appeared more and more frequently among the clerics.

In time, the amalgamation and elaboration of these playlets put a considerable strain on church facilities and on the religious ceremonies themselves. The plays became so complicated as to be distracting, and the crowds so large as to be difficult to accommodate inside the churches, large though most of them were. Gradually, moreover, the dramatizations came to include more and more of the comic and secular elements that inevitably crept into them, however soberly they had originally been intended. Members of the lower clergy were often guilty, apparently, of offending in favor of satire and broad comic effects: the villainous Herod was frequently applauded, and stories like that of Balaam and his ass took on a distinctly farcical flavor. The official reaction to the problem was erratic. In 1207 Pope Innocent III issued a decree forbidding the use of masks in church and prohibiting the Feast of Fools, an annual burlesque of religious ceremony and officialdom; but the order did not clearly denounce liturgical plays; other officials, meanwhile, took local actions that served to discourage or curtail activity. But the sum total of the criticism against this drama and of the legislation passed to control or prohibit it seems not to have greatly affected its progress. It continued to develop and to flourish into the fourteenth century, when as a result of many factors it gradually and discontinuously moved out of the churches, sometimes to church porches or more frequently to town squares. The one piece of legislation that doubtless encouraged this movement was Pope Urban IV's institution of the Feast of Corpus Christi in 1264: this holiday in honor of the sacrament offered a subject to which almost any of the liturgical plays was relevant; and, since it is celebrated eight and a half weeks after Easter, it offered better weather for the production of plays out-of-doors. Gradually, Corpus Christi became the focal occasion for dramatic presentations.

THE MIRACLE CYCLES Under these new conditions the liturgical drama underwent a number of different but for the most part parallel developments. Everywhere Latin gradually gave way to the vernacular, and the clergy gradually yielded its functions as writers, producers, and actors to the laity, until the plays and their production became almost exclusively the business of secular groups. In Italy the plays tended to become the property of lay religious organizations and in France of cities or townships, while in England they tended to become the property of particular craft guilds. They continued to be re-written, adapted, and amplified, drawing on all of the materials of the Bible and much of the material of saints' lives; by the fourteenth century most of the elaborate single plays now extant had achieved a relatively final form, and by the early fifteenth most of the great cycles of plays were complete. Certain distinctions are evident here. Italy developed no cycles of plays and tended to hold to a relatively learned standard of writing, probably because the clergy there continued to take a considerable part in the activity, while France and England tended to develop cycles of plays, among them a number of highly elaborate and famous ones, and tended to a more popular standard of writing suggestive of the wider participation of the laity. Altogether, at least three distinctive styles of play production developed, each peculiarly adapted to the plays of particular communities; though it is difficult to sustain firm national distinctions in this matter.

Although England could boast all three modes of production, France was by far the more famous for the system of simultaneous stages consisting of a series of platforms, or stations, arranged around a town square. Designed for the production of cycles of plays of some complexity, this system provided a separate fixed station for each of the plays comprising the cycle. If the cycle happened to deal with the Nativity, one station might be designed for the play of the Annunciation, another for the one in which the shepherds sight the star, another for a play laid in the court of one of the wise men, and still another for the Nativity itself. If the cycle dealt with the Easter story, successive stations would be designed for successive episodes in the passion, crucifixion, and resurrection of Christ. Usually, the member plays of the cycle were staged in sequence so that the crowd could move from one station to the next as the story unfolded. In time, certain communities became famous for the pattern in which they arranged their stations: Valenciennes was celebrated for its straight-line method of presentation on a single platform, and Mons for its semicircular arrangement of the sixty-seven stations needed for its *Mystery of the Passion*. In England the plays from the *Ludus Coventriae* are thought to have been performed on stations.

By far the more usual mode of production in England, however, was the processional method using pageant wagons. The pageant or miracle wagon was a long, rectangular box mounted on wheels and drawn by horses. It consisted, usually, of two stories, a lower covered by curtains which served as the off-stage area, and an upper open to view which served as the playing surface. On this playing surface there might be two or three shallow platforms indicating different locales to be used in the play. Usually each of the member plays comprising a cycle was assigned to a single pageant wagon, and the cycle was presented by drawing the wagons in their narrative order to prearranged locations in the town, where they were halted and the plays were performed. In this way the spectators had only to station themselves at one of the prearranged points of performance to see the whole cycle as the wagons were brought up in their turns. Most of the great English Miracle Cycles were presented in this way.

Less well known, though in use both in England and France, was the method of production that made use of rounds. The "round" was a flat, circular, open place, constructed so that a large circle was enclosed either by a wall or a moat. On the periphery of the circle, but inside it, a number of towers were built, providing elevated platforms for separate locales, and in the center of the circle was the main tower or stage. The audience arranged itself inside the circle, leaving passageways from the peripheral towers to the center, and the actors moved from tower to tower as the action required. In England this mode of production was used for a wide variety of plays, most notably the Cornish Miracle Cycle.

By using one or the other of these production methods, medieval communities were capable of mounting cycles of plays of tremendous length and complexity. Unfortunately, not very much is known about other aspects of production. From records we know that the sets erected on the stations or on the wagons were on some occasions highly elaborate and on others simple to the point of bareness: the mouth of Hell might be a construction of great intricacy, while certain locales might be indicated simply by a throne designating a palace, a spinning wheel designating a cottage, or simply a little sign announcing a place. Costumes on the whole were contemporary: princes of however great antiquity tended to look like medieval princes and commoners like medieval peasants. Such practice is understandable, of course, when we remember that the personnel recruited for set construction and stage work of other kinds, including the acting, were for the most part ordinary citizens, members of guilds or other local organizations, in other words, amateurs who once a year turned to the communal project of producing their cycle of plays. Except for the occasional professional recruited from the minstrelsy for a major role, accordingly, the acting too must have been relatively simple and primitive. Yet it would probably be a mistake to imagine that it was ineffective: the example of such surviving traditions as we have—the *Passion* presented at Oberammergau, for example—suggests how far devotion and commitment could take these communities toward high artistic achievement.

Generically, the plays produced are known as mystery or miracle plays and the cycles as mystery or miracle cycles. In England, where the word "mystery" applied to "craft" or "trade" rather than to a religious meaning, the terms were interchangeable, though in fact "miracle" was the more widely used until quite late; but in France "mystery" usually designated those plays deriving from Bible story, while "miracle" served for those deriving from saints' lives. Structurally, the plays are unique in the history of western drama. Most of them were ultimately derived from earlier liturgical plays in Latin which in the course of time had been translated and revised by several hands. Since the Bible stories and stories of saints' lives permitted few, if any, departures, the playwrights were restricted for the most part to shaping the material by means of omissions or emphasis rather than by additions of invented material. The playwrights' aim, after all, was to clarify the fixed interpretation of the story and to embolden the qualities traditionally found in it, and they usually accomplished these purposes by pointing contrasts already present in the materials and solidifying moments already well known. Only in the latest, most highly developed examples do we find a judicious and imaginative use of invented materials to heighten the traditional power and meaning of the story. Because the Bible stories were so well known, moreover, the treatment of them was distinctly episodic: although the cycles followed the narrative thread of the Bible, or of some part of it like the passion, they did so at some distance, skipping great blocks of material because it was assumed that the audience could easily fill in the gaps. By these general methods cycles were assembled that dealt with the whole story of man, from the creation to the last judgment, or with some segment of material like episodes from the passion or the Ascension.

The story of medieval drama in France is long and distinguished. One of the earliest extant plays in French, the anonymous *Mystery of Adam* (*c.*1180) in Anglo-Norman, is also one of the best. With its amalgamation of several stories within a single structure, it clearly illustrates the liturgical tendency of linking actions episodically, yet with its noisy devils and fulsome spectacular effects it at the same time exemplifies the process of secularization. With secularization the plays gradually passed into the hands of lay organizations, until by the first quarter of the fourteenth century they were largely the responsibility of trade guilds and secular confraternities.

The confraternities have a rather special place in the story of French drama both in the Middle Ages and beyond, and one of them, the Confraternity of the Passion in Paris, was long a key element in the growth of theatrical activity in the capital. Typically they were societies of mutual aid with a membership consisting largely of tradesmen, but frequently including professional entertainers, and normally they produced mystery and miracle plays, as in some communities trade guilds continued to do, as part of the street festivals on Corpus Christi. The Confraternity of the Passion in Paris was distinctive in that in 1402 it received from the King a monopoly on public and private performances in the city and its environs. For nearly a century and a half the monopoly meant little more than that the Confraternity was authorized to continue producing its elaborate *Mystery of the Passion* in rented public buildings in and around the city, and, in fact, during this period its contribution to the tradition was probably less important than that of more brilliant sponsoring organizations in provincial cities like Metz, Saumur, Arras, Valenciennes, and Dieppe. Only in the second half of the sixteenth century, when the monopoly became a serious impediment to the development of theatrical activity in Paris, did it take up a crucial role in the story of French drama, and then, as we shall see, largely as a restrictive force.

In addition to the confraternities and trade guilds, meanwhile, certain other organizations, also numerous and dispersed, specialized in the production of farces and morality plays. Although France's rich tradition in farce traces to the same carnival origins that underlie farce everywhere in Europe, for convenience historians usually date it from the remarkable work of Adam de la Halle (*c.*1240–*c.*1288), *The Play of the Greenery* (*c.*1276). Thereafter, a tradition of short, rowdy comedies in octosyllabic couplets emerges—rather dimly in the fourteenth century, but distinctly in the fifteenth and sixteenth centuries. These plays were produced by companies or associations of players which in most major cities were responsible for the organization of civic feasts and celebrations for such occasions as May Day or carnival. Such groups, consisting of from a dozen to several hundred members, drew their personnel from all levels of society and, like the Cornards of Evreux, the Infanterie of Dijon, or the Basoche (a guild of law-clerks in Paris), frequently had long and distinguished histories. It is thought that the well-known farce *Maître Pierre Pathelin* (*c.*1464) was written for a production by the Basoche; Andrieu de la Vigne's hybrid farce-miracle, *The Miracle of the Blind Man and the Cripple* (1496) was written for a comparable organization in Seurre.

In England we have evidence that miracle plays were produced in from forty to fifty communities and three practically complete cycles of considerable size. The cycles date roughly from the second quarter of the fifteenth century, and the longest, the York Cycle, contains forty-eight plays covering the whole history of mankind and required several days to play in its entirety. Consisting of member plays that vary in length from short pieces of a single scene to longer, multi-scene structures of surprising delicacy and subtlety, the York Cycle is memorable for the grace of its poetry, the sober dignity of its pervasive tone, and its occasional glimpses of a grim reality faithfully reproduced. Its powerful *Crucifixion,* for example, combines a protracted representation of the details of the crucifixion with a subtle confrontation of the redeemed and the redeemer in such a way as to imply both an almost primitive interest in detail for its sensational value and a high order of dramatic imagination. The achievement of the play, as of so many of these plays, lies in its capacity to reconcile these rather disparate levels of writing by means of an overriding and unifying purpose to celebrate the God depicted and the religion implied. Like the York Cycle, the Chester Cycle represented all of human history, but did so in plays rather more varied in tone and more overtly didactic in purpose. It consists of twenty-five plays and is notable for its lively digressions into comedy and its use of such mechanical effects as spirits suspended in the air. Two rather unusual facts about it are that it was probably not produced at Corpus Christi but at Whitsuntide (the week beginning about 50 days after Easter) and that its plays have traditionally been associated with one author, the local monk Ranulf Higden (*fl.*1350). Although Higden's authorship is by no means clear, his is one of the few names to survive of the hundreds of playwrights from this period.

But it is the Wakefield Cycle, comprising thirty-two plays, which reveals the miracle play in England in its most fully developed form: a form characterized not only by the most extensive additions of invented material and the boldest departures from traditional treatment, but also by the most successful accommodations of traditional elements to the end of celebration. Like the other cycles, it too deals with all of human history; but here whole episodes have been re-shaped for comic effect, as in the *Cain and Abel,* and some plays have been very nearly converted into social documents by an extraordinary attention to Yorkshire backgrounds and Yorkshire types. These qualities are especially clear in the five plays of the anonymous playwright now known as the Wakefield Master. Although he is usually identified by his characteristic stanzaic form, he is equally unmistakable in his skillful rendering of backgrounds and his unfailing eye for satiric and humorous detail. The strategy of lending texture, focus, and depth to traditional episodes by supplementing the traditional materials with pertinent invented matter was taken by him as far as it was to go in this drama. Where in his *Noah* he deepened the meaning of the play by adding the delightful scenes in which Noah's intractable wife refuses to enter the ark, in his *Second Shepherds' Play* he focussed almost exclusively on the invented material concerning Mak, the shepherds, and the episode of the false birth, only at the last moment juxtaposing it boldly, almost impiously, to the Nativity story.

By comparison with our own drama, even the Wakefield plays with their rather coarse-grained verse and their simple and bold adaptation of means to the end or glorification seem rather primitive. But the rough-hewn quality of much of this drama should not be allowed to obscure its intrinsic merit. Despite the Reformation and the increased hostility to these plays because of their Catholic origins, they continued to be produced in England even into Shakespeare's day.

THE MORALITY TRADITION After the miracle play, the other medieval dramatic form of distinguished tradition was the morality play. The origins of the morality play are obscure. Although frequently tied to the rise of Protestantism, with its emphasis on the salvation of the individual soul, it appears to derive from a little-understood fusion of a number of traditional medieval forms. Clearly it owed a great deal to medieval allegory and to the allegorical method originating in Prudentius' *Psychomachia* (5th century A.D.) and widely practised in works like *The Romance of the Rose* (13th century). Just as clearly it borrowed something from the medieval homilies and such argumentative forms as the *débat*. Moreover, as a dramatic form it is thought to owe still something else to the Pater Noster Plays, plays commemorating the power of the Lord's Prayer that are known to have existed in York, Beverly, and Lincoln, but about which information is scant. In any event, by an obscure assimilation of these forms, the morality play emerged in the late fourteenth century and achieved a firm footing by the first quarter of the fifteenth. Although there are traces of it on the continent, it survives primarily in some thirty examples from England.

Structurally, morality plays are seldom more than dramatic sermons which put several abstract characters through an action which allegorically illustrates the thesis to be sustained. One character might be the body and another the soul, in which case the play would represent their struggle as a kind of abstract of the drama of salvation. Among the most frequent subjects in the moralities, in fact, were the summons of death and the contention for man's soul that follows, the combat between the spirits of good and evil for dominion over man, and the debate between body and soul. As dramatic compositions, these plays marked certain advances over the miracle play. They were usually longer and more complex and they went beyond the traditional story by requiring the playwright to devise an original action with which to illustrate orthodox doctrine. Without a Bible story to guide and constrain him, the playwright had to invent situations which, because of the nature of the subjects treated, were characteristically rich in conflict. Although in actual fact the morality plays that remain are on the whole rather heavy and dull, they established important precedents by enlarging significantly, among other things, the function of the playwright.

In England the moralities enjoyed their greatest popularity in the fifteenth and sixteenth centuries. Apparently they were produced, not on religious holidays exclusively, but at almost any time, and their production embraced a wide variety of physical conditions and production methods. One of the earliest and most complex, *The Castle of Perseverance* dates from about 1425, and from an extant manuscript setting forth the elaborate plan of its production we know that it was played by the system of the medieval round. More frequently, the moralities were played in the halls of noble houses or on temporary scaffolds of planks mounted on carpenter's horses in innyards. These methods were favored by the small professional companies of players that in England were beginning to appear during this period and that were elusively linked with the history of the morality play. It was probably they who developed the symbolic costumes by which abstract characters, each with his characteristic color and emblem, were readily identified, and they who amplified progressively the comic element typically met in the devil's aides and most notably in a well known diabolical emissary known as the "Vice."

Of the authors of the earliest moralities, including the best, *Everyman* (*c.*1475), we know almost nothing. For the most part they were probably clerics who seized upon the form as yet another device for teaching the invariable lessons of Christian doctrine. Yet the form was not long in revealing its great adaptability. By about 1475 it had been sufficiently contaminated by vulgar comic elements in a work like *Mankind* to mark some decline, and in the sixteenth century it was appropriated by writers of all kinds as they realized its suitability for controversy. In the struggle between the Protestants and the Catholics it was used by both sides, to represent the Protestants in plays like *The Treachery of Papists* (*c*.1520) and the Catholics in plays like *Hycke-Scorner* (*c*.1515). In politics it was used by John Skelton in his *Magnificence* (*c*.1520) and by John Roos in his *Lord Goveraunce* (*c*.1527), a play for which both the author and the actors spent some time in prison. In the same way it was appropriated by humanist writers and bent to the purpose of learned controversy in works like John Rastell's *The Four Elements* (*c*.1510) and Henry Medwall's *Nature* (*c*.1500). But somehow the learning and sophistication that were brought to the form when cultivated men began to use it for propagandistic purposes never succeeded as the simpler devotion and passion of earlier writers had succeeded in plays like *Everyman*. By the middle of the sixteenth century, when the plays had become almost the exclusive property of the small troupes of professional players, the form was so hybrid a mixture as to be difficult to distinguish from farce. Like the miracle plays, the moralities survived into the age of Shakespeare, when they yielded to more generous and ambitious conceptions of dramatic structure, and by this time their dramatic method and their distinctive didactic bias were deeply ingrained in the English dramatic tradition.

Bibliography

Roman Drama and Theater:

Allen, J. T., *Stage Antiquities of the Greeks and Romans and Their Influence,* New York, 1927.

Beare, William, *The Roman Stage; A Short History of Latin Drama in the Time of the Republic,* 2nd ed., London, 1955.

Bieber, Margarete, *The History of the Greek and Roman Theater,* 2nd ed., Princeton, N.J., 1961.

Coleman-Norton, P. R., "Philosophical Aspects of Early Roman Comedy," *Classical Philology,* XXXI (1936), 320–337.

Duckworth, George E., *The Nature of Roman Comedy,* Princeton, N.J., 1952.

Duff, J. W., *The Literary History of Rome:* Vol. I, *From the Origins to the Close of the Golden Age,* Rev. and ed. by A. M. Duff, New York, 1953.

Hamilton, Edith, *The Roman Way,* New York, 1932.

Hanson, J. A., *Roman Theater-Temples,* Princeton, N.J., 1959.

Harsh, Philip W., *A Handbook of Classical Drama,* Stanford, Calif., 1944.

Moulton, R. G., *The Ancient Classical Drama: A Study in Literary Evolution,* 2nd ed., Oxford, 1898.

Norwood, Gilbert, *Plautus and Terence,* New York, 1932.

Saunders, C., *Costume in Roman Comedy,* New York, 1909.

Thomson, J. A. K., *The Classical Background of English Literature,* London, 1948.

Medieval Drama and Theater:

Bates, K. L., *English Religious Drama,* New York, 1904.

Bevington, David M., *From Mankind to Marlowe,* Cambridge, Mass., 1962.

Cady, F. W., "The Wakefield Group in Towneley," *Journal of English and Germanic Philology,* XI (1912), 244–266.

Cargill, Oscar, *Drama and Liturgy,* New York, 1930.

Chambers, E. K., *The English Folk-Play,* Oxford, 1933.

———, *The Medieval Stage,* 2 Vols., Oxford, 1903.

Cosbey, Robert C., "The Mak Story and Its Folklore Analogues," *Speculum,* XX (1945), 310–317.

Craig, Hardin, *English Religious Drama of the Middle Ages,* Oxford, 1955.

Farnham, Willard, *The Medieval Heritage of Elizabethan Tragedy,* Berkeley, Calif., 1936.

Frank, Grace, *The Medieval French Drama,* Oxford, 1954.

Gardiner, Harold C., *Mysteries' End: An Investigation of the Last Days of the Medieval Religious Stage,* New Haven, Conn., 1946.

Hunningher, Benjamin, *The Origin of the Theater,* New York, 1961.

MacKenzie, W. Roy, *The English Moralities From the Point of View of Allegory,* Boston, 1914.

Marshall, M. H., "The Dramatic Tradition Established by the Liturgical Plays," *PMLA,* LVI (1941), 962–991.

Nicoll, Allardyce, *Masks, Mimes, and Miracles,* New York, 1931.

Rossiter, A. P., *English Drama From Early Times to the Elizabethans; Its Background, Origins, and Development,* New York, 1950.

Salter, F. M., *Medieval Drama in Chester,* Toronto, 1955.

Southern, Richard, *The Medieval Theatre in the Round,* London, 1957.

Stratman, Carl J., *Bibliography of Medieval Drama,* Berkeley, Calif., 1954.

Stuart, D. C., *Stage Decoration in France in the Middle Ages,* New York, 1910.

Wickham, Glynne, *Early English Stages, 1300–1660,* 2 Vols., New York, 1959–62.

Williams, Arnold, *The Drama of Medieval England,* East Lansing, Mich., 1961.

Young, Karl, *The Drama of the Medieval Church,* 2 Vols., Oxford, 1933.

Masked mummers, from a 14th-century miniature.
Photo Historical Pictures Service—Chicago

Plautus

Titus Maccius Plautus (*c.254–184* B.C.) *wrote the earliest complete works in Latin literature now extant. Although he almost certainly knew hardship and poverty, very little is known about his life beyond that he acquired an intimate knowledge of the theater at an early age and wrote probably some 48 plays, of which 21 survive. A practical playwright bent on pleasing the rowdy audiences of his day, Plautus composed his comedies by freely adapting one or more Greek New Comedies to the conditions of contemporary Rome in a dramatic form known as the* Fabula Palliata. *To the grace and urbanity of his sources he brought great liveliness of farcical movement and pungency of verbal style. Soon after his death he was widely accepted as the classic writer of farce.*

Chronology

*c.*254 B.C. Probable year of his birth at Sarsina in Umbria.

235–25 Probable period during which he came to Rome and began working in the theater, most likely as an actor in *Atellanae* farces.

225–15 According to legend, lost money in speculations and worked for a time in a mill.

212–07 Probable period of his *Asinaria,* or *The Comedy of Asses.*

205 Probable year of his production of the *Miles Gloriosus,* or *The Braggart Warrior.*

200 Wrote his *Stichus.*

191 Wrote his *Pseudolus.*

188 Probable year of his production of the *Trinummus,* or *The Three Penny Day.*

185 Probable year of his production of the *Casina.*

184 Died in Rome.

Selected Bibliography

Beare, William, "Plautus and His Public," *Classical Review,* XLII (1928), 106–111.

Blancké, W. W., *The Dramatic Values in Plautus,* Geneva, N.Y., 1918.

Collins, W. L., *Plautus and Terence,* Edinburgh, 1873.

Coulter, C. C., "The Plautine Tradition in Shakespeare," *Journal of English and Germanic Philology,* XIX (1920), 66–83.

Hough, J. N., "The Development of Plautus' Art," *Classical Philology,* XXX (1935), 43–57.

Juniper, W. H., "Character Portrayal in Plautus," *Classical Journal,* XXXI (1935–36), 276–288.

Norwood, Gilbert, *Plautus and Terence,* New York, 1932.

Prescott, H. W., "The Interpretation of Roman Comedy," *Classical Philology,* XI (1916), 125–147.

Westaway, K. M., *The Original Element in Plautus,* Cambridge, 1917.

Wieland, Helen Emma, *Deception in Plautus: A Study in the Technique of Roman Comedy,* Boston, 1920.

Wright, F. A., *Three Roman Poets. Plautus, Catullus, Ovid. Their Times and Work,* New York, 1938.

Masked comic actor. Roman sculpture.
Photo Radio Times Hulton Picture Library

THE TWIN MENAECHMI

by Plautus

Translated by Bonnell Thornton and Richard Warner
Revised by Anthony Caputi

Characters

MENAECHMUS, *of Epidamnum*
OLD MAN, *father-in-law of* MENAECHMUS
PENICULUS, *a Parasite, a Hanger-on to* MENAECHMUS
SERVANT *of* MENAECHMUS
PHYSICIAN
CYLINDRUS, *a Cook*
MENAECHMUS SOSICLES, *of Syracuse*
MESSENIO, *Servant of* MENAECHMUS SOSICLES
WIFE *of Menaechmus of Epidamnum*
MAID-SERVANT *of Menaechmus of Epidamnum*
EROTIUM, *a Courtezan, Mistress of Menaechmus of Epidamnum*
Servants of Menaechmus of Epidamnum

Epidamnum, a city of Macedonia

Prologue

Spectators—first and foremost—may all health
And happiness attend both you and me!
I bring you Plautus, but with tongue, not hand;
Give him, I pray, a fair and gentle hearing.
Now learn the argument and lend attention: 5
I'll be as brief as may be. 'Tis the way
With poets in their comedies to feign
The business pass'd at Athens so that you
May think it the more Grecian. For our play,
I'll not pretend the incidents to happen   10
Where they do not: the argument is Grecian,
And yet it is not Attic, but Sicilian.*
So much by way of preface to our tale,
Which now I'll deal out to you in full measure,
Not as it were by bushels or by pecks;   15
I'll pour before you the whole granary,

---

12 That is, in the Greek spoken in Sicily.

So much am I inclined to tell the plot.
There was a certain merchant, an old man
Of Syracuse. He had two sons were twins,
So like in form and feature that the nurse
Could not distinguish them who gave them suck,
Nor ev'n the mother that had brought them forth,
This one inform'd me who had seen the children;
Myself ne'er saw them, don't imagine it.
When the boys were sev'n years old, the father
Freighted a vessel with much store of merchandize,
Put one of them on board, and took the child
Along with him to traffic at Tarentum.*
The other with his mother he left at home.
When they arrived there at this same Tarentum,
It happen'd there were sports; and multitudes,
As they are wont at shows, were got together.
In the crowd the child stray'd from his father.
There chanc'd to be a certain merchant there,
An Epidamnian, who pick'd up the boy
And bore him home with him to Epidamnum.
The father, on the sad loss of his boy,
Took it to heart most heavily and died
For grief of't some days after at Tarentum.
When news of this affair was brought to Syracuse
Unto the grandfather, how that the child
Was stolen and the father dead with grief,
The good old man changed the other's name,
So much he lov'd the one that had been stolen:
Him that was left at home he calls Menaechmus,
Which was the other's name; and by the same
The grandsire too was call'd; I do remember it
Readily for I heard him called for.
I now forewarn you, lest you err hereafter,
Both the twin brothers bear the self-same name.
But I must foot it back to Epidamnum
That I may clear this matter up exactly.
If any of you here have any business
At Epidamnum you want done, speak out,
You may command me—but on this condition:
Give me the money to defray the charges.
He that don't give it will be much mistaken;
Much more mistaken will he be that does.

But now am I return'd whence I set forth,
Though yet I stand here in the self-same place.
This Epidamnian whom I spoke of, he
Who stole that other boy, no children had

---

[28] A city in southern Italy, once a Greek colony.

Except his riches; therefore he adopts
This stranger-boy, gives him a wife well-portioned,
And makes him his sole heir, before he died.   65
Then as he was going to the country,
After a heavy rain, trying to ford
A rapid river near the city,
Th' rapid river knocked him off his legs
And snatch'd him to destruction. A large fortune   70
Fell to the youth, who now lives here; the other
Who dwells at Syracuse is come to-day
To Epidamnum with a slave of his
In quest of his twin brother. Now this city (*Pointing to the scenes*)
Is Epidamnum while the play is acting;   75
And when another shall be represented,
'Twill be another place just as our company
Are also wont to shift their characters.
As you know the same player is now a pimp,
And then a young gallant, an old curmudgeon,   80
A poor man, rich man, parasite, or priest.

Act One

Scene 1

(*Enter* PENICULUS, *the Parasite*)

PENICULUS*   Our young men call me *dishcloth* for this reason,
Whene'er I eat I wipe the tables clean.
Now in my judgment they act foolishly
Who bind in chains their captives, and clap fetters
Upon their run-away slaves: for if you heap   5
Evil on evil to torment the wretch,
The stronger his desire is to escape.
They'll free them from their chains by any means:
Load them with gifts, they file away the door,
Or knock the bolt out with a stone. 'Tis vain this: 10
But would you keep a man from 'scaping from you,
Be sure you chain him fast with meat and drink
And tie him by the beak to a full table.
Give him his fill, allow him meat and drink
At pleasure, in abundance, every day,   15
And I'll be sworn, although his crime be capital,
He will not run away: you'll easily
Secure him when you bind him with these bonds.
They're wondrous supple these same belly-bonds,
The more you stretch them, they will bind the harder.   20

---

¹ The word means "sponge" or "tail" since the tails of foxes or oxen were used as sponges for cleaning tables.

For instance, I'm now going to Menaechmus,
Most willingly I'm going to be bound,
According to his sentence past upon me.
Good soul! he's not content with giving us
A bare support and meagre sustenance,   25
But crams us even to satiety;
Gives us, as 'twere, new life, when dead with hunger.
O he's a rare physician: he's a youth
Of lordly appetite; he treats most daintily;
His table's bravely served—such heaps of dishes,   30
You must stand on your couch to reach the top.
Yet I've some days been absent from his house;
Homely I've liv'd at home with my *dear* ones,
For all I eat or buy is *dear* to me,
Yet they desert the very ones that rais'd them.   35
Now will I visit him. But the door opens,
And see! Menaechmus' self is coming forth.

Scene 2

(*Enter* MENAECHMUS *of Epidamnum, carrying a robe and speaking to his
wife within*)

M. EPIDAMNUM   Were you not good for nothing, were you not   40
An ass, a stubborn idiot, what you saw
Displeas'd your husband would displease you too.
From this day forward, if you use me thus,
I'll turn you out of doors and send you back
A widow to your father; for whenever   45
I would go forth, you hold me, call me back,
Ask where I'm going, what 'tis I'm about,
And what's my business, what I want abroad.
I've married sure some officer o' the customs,
I'm so examin'd—what I've done—what do.   50
Too kindly you've been treated hitherto;
I'll tell you how you shall be—since I allow you
Maids, jewels, cloths, wool, since you want for nothing.
If you were wife, you'd dread the consequence
And cease to watch your husband, and that you   55
May watch me to some purpose for your pains
I'll dine abroad now with some trull or other.

PENICULUS   (*Aside*) He means to gall his wife by what he says;
But me he spites, for if he dine abroad,
On me he recks his vengeance, not on her.   60

M. EPIDAMNUM   Victoria! by my tauntings, I at last
Have driven her from the door. Where, where are all,
The intriguing husbands? why do they delay

To bring me gifts, and thank me for my prowess?
I've stol'n this robe here of my wife's and mean   65
To carry it to my mistress. So we ought
To trick these crafty husband-watching dames.
'Tis a fair action, this of mine, 'tis right,
'Tis pleasant, faith, and admirably carried.
With plague enough, I've ta'en it from one plague   70
To give it to another. Thus I've gain'd
A booty from the foe without our loss.

PENICULUS   (*Aloud*) What portion of the booty's mine, young Sir?

M. EPIDAMNUM   Undone! I'm fall'n into an ambuscade.

PENICULUS   You've lighted on a safeguard; never fear.   75

M. EPIDAMNUM   Who's that?

PENICULUS   'Tis I.

M. EPIDAMNUM   O my most welcome friend,
Save you.

PENICULUS   And you.   80

M. EPIDAMNUM   How fares it?

PENICULUS   Let me take
My genius by the hand.

M. EPIDAMNUM   You could not come
More opportune than now.   85

PENICULUS   It is my way:
I know to hit each point and nick of time.

M. EPIDAMNUM   Shall I acquaint you with a saucy prank?

PENICULUS   Saucy? What cook has drest it? I shall know
If he has marr'd it when I see the relics.   90

M. EPIDAMNUM   Now prithee tell me, have you never seen
The picture of an eagle bearing off
Jove's Ganymede, or *Venus* with *Adonis?*

PENICULUS   Ay, many a time. But what are they to me?

M. EPIDAMNUM   Look at me. Do I bear resemblance to them?   95

PENICULUS   What means that robe?

M. EPIDAMNUM   Call me a clever fellow.

PENICULUS   Where shall we dine?

M. EPIDAMNUM   Poh, say what I command you.

PENICULUS   Well then,—thou art a clever fellow.   100

M. EPIDAMNUM   What,
Canst add nought of thy own?

PENICULUS   Yes, a joyous fellow.

M. EPIDAMNUM   Proceed.

PENICULUS   Not I, i' faith, unless I know   105
Why there's a falling out 'twixt you and Madam.
I take great care to have this from yourself.

M. EPIDAMNUM   Tell me without the knowledge of my wife,
Where shall we kill, where bury, time?

PENICULUS   Come, come; 110
   You say right; I will dig its grave. The day's
   Already half-expired.
M. EPIDAMNUM   'Tis all delay,
   Your chattering thus.
PENICULUS   Knock out my only eye, 115
   Menaechmus, if I speak one other word
   But what you bid.
M. EPIDAMNUM   Draw hither from the door.
PENICULUS   I will.
M. EPIDAMNUM   Draw hither. 120
PENICULUS   Well.
M. EPIDAMNUM   Come quickly hither,
   Come from the lioness's den.
PENICULUS   'Fore heav'n,
   You'd make a dext'rous charioteer. 125
M. EPIDAMNUM   Why so?
PENICULUS   You look behind you, lest your wife should follow.
M. EPIDAMNUM   What say you now?
PENICULUS   What say I? what you will
   I say and unsay. 130
M. EPIDAMNUM   Were your nose to any thing,
   Could you not make a shrewd guess by the smell?
PENICULUS   Aye, surely: the whole college, Sir, of Augurs
   Have not so quick a scent at divination.
M. EPIDAMNUM   Come then, and smell this robe which I have here. 135
   What does it smell of? (*holding it up*) won't you take it?
PENICULUS   Hey day!
   A woman's garment should be smelt at top;
   The scent is else too strong for any nose.
M. EPIDAMNUM   Come, smell it here then, good Peniculus. 140
   How you make faces at it!
PENICULUS   I can't help it.
M. EPIDAMNUM   What does it smell of? answer.
PENICULUS   It smells strong
   Of theft, of whore, and dinner. 145
M. EPIDAMNUM   I'm now going
   To carry it to my mistress, my Erotium.
   I'll bid her to provide a dinner for us—
   For me, for you, and for herself: we'll there
   Carouse it till the morrow's morning star. 150
PENICULUS   O bravely spoken!—shall I knock?
M. EPIDAMNUM   You may.
   Yet hold a while.
PENICULUS   The cup was just at hand;
   'Tis now a thousand paces off. 155
M. EPIDAMNUM   Knock softly.

PENICULUS Are you afraid the door is made of crockery?

M. EPIDAMNUM Hold, prithee, hold—herself is coming forth.

PENICULUS Oh, Sir, you look upon the sun; your eyes
     Are blinded with her brightness.   160

Scene 3

(*Enter* EROTIUM)

EROTIUM My *Menaechmus*!
     My love! good morrow!

PENICULUS Won't you welcome me too?

EROTIUM You rank not in the number of my friends.   165

PENICULUS Yet treat me as a supernumerary.*

M. EPIDAMNUM We mean to pitch a battle with you today.

EROTIUM Aye, that we will.

M. EPIDAMNUM And prove, with pitcher fill'd,
     Which is the mightier warrior at the bowl.   170
     Yourself shall be commander; you shall choose
     Which you will pass the night with. O my sweet,
     When I look on you, how I loathe my wife!

EROTIUM And yet you cannot choose, but you must wrap you
     In some part of her gear. Pray what is this?   175

M. EPIDAMNUM A cast skin of my wife's to be slipt on
     By thee, my rose-bud.

EROTIUM You've the readiest way
     To win preëminence in my affection
     Of all who pay me suit.   180

PENICULUS Right harlot this!
     A harlot's sure to coax whene'er she finds
     There's any thing to get. If you loved him,
     You would have bit his nose off by this time
     With flobbering.   185

M. EPIDAMNUM Take my cloak, Peniculus;
     For I must dedicate the spoils I've vow'd.

PENICULUS (*Putting the robe on him*) But prithee now, you'll afterwards
     Dance in your robe?

M. EPIDAMNUM I dance in't?—You are mad.   190

PENICULUS Are you or I most mad? Well, if you won't,
     Then pull it off.

M. EPIDAMNUM I ran a mighty risk
     In stealing of this robe; in my mind truly
     Young Hercules ran not an equal hazard when   195
     He spoil'd the bold *Hippolita* of her girdle. (*Giving the robe to* EROTIUM)
     Take it, since you alone of women living
     Suit your affection gently unto mine.

EROTIUM True lovers should be thus disposed.

---

[166] A soldier held in reserve and normally denied the privileges of regular soldiers.

PENICULUS Provided
    They would run headlong into beggary.
M. EPIDAMNUM 'Tis not a year past, since it cost me
    Four *minae* for my wife.
PENICULUS Four *minae,* then,
    By your account, are plainly gone for ever.
M. EPIDAMNUM Know you what I would have you do?
EROTIUM I know,
    And will take care according to your wish.
M. EPIDAMNUM Let dinner be provided for us three;
    Send to the market for some dainty morsel,
    A gammon, some sow's kernels, a hog's cheek,
    Or sausages, or something of that kind,
    Which, when they're brought to table, may suggest
    A hawk-like appetite. About it straight.
EROTIUM I' faith I will.
M. EPIDAMNUM We're going to the Forum.
    We'll be back directly; while 'tis dressing,
    We will amuse us with a bite i' th' interim.
EROTIUM Come when you will, dear; all things shall be ready.
M. EPIDAMNUM Quick, follow me.
PENICULUS Yes, yes, I'll have an eye to you,
    Close at your heels, I warrant; I'll not lose you,
    Not for the wealth of all the gods. (*Exeunt* MENAECHMUS *and* PENICULUS)
EROTIUM Call forth
    The cook Cylindrus, bid him come this instant.

Scene 4

(*Enter* CYLINDRUS)

EROTIUM Take the hand-basket, and, d'ye mind? here are
    Three pieces for you. See you hold them well.
CYLINDRUS I will.
EROTIUM Go to the market and provide
    Enough for three; and let there be sufficient,
    But nought to spare.
CYLINDRUS What kind of guests, pray, are they?
EROTIUM I, and Menaechmus, and his parasite.
CYLINDRUS Nay, there are ten then, for the parasite
    Will lay about him equal to eight men.
EROTIUM I've told you what's the number of our guests:
    You will provide accordingly.
CYLINDRUS I warrant.
    'Tis cooked already: you've but to sit down.
EROTIUM You'll come back quickly.
CYLINDRUS In an instant.

Act Two

Scene 1

(*Enter* MENAECHMUS SOSICLES, *and* MESSENIO, *his Servant*)

M. SOSICLES   No greater joy have voyagers, Messenio,
   Than from the far off deep to spy out land.

MESSENIO   To speak the truth, 'tis still a greater joy
   To find that land, when you arrive, your country.   5
   But wherefore come we now to Epidamnum?
   Must we go round each island, like the sea?

M. SOSICLES   I am searching my twin brother.

MESSENIO   Good now,
   When will there be an end of searching for him?   10
   This is the sixth year since we set about it;
   The Istrians, the Illyrians, the Massilians,*
   The Spaniards, the whole Adriatic gulf,
   With farthest Greece and each Italian coast
   That the sea washes, have we sailed around.   15
   Had we been looking for a needle, sure
   We should have found it long ago, if visible.
   Thus we seek a dead man 'mong the living;
   When we have found him, were he living.

M. SOSICLES   Would I could find out one that might assure me   20
   Of his own knowledge that my brother's dead!
   Then I'd forego my quest, not otherwise.
   But while I live I'll never spare my pains,
   Nor ever will desist from seeking him.
   How dear he's to my heart, too well I feel—   25

MESSENIO   You in a bull-rush seek a knot—'tis vain.*
   Come, let's return, unless you mean to write
   A book of voyages.

M. SOSICLES   No fine, subtle speeches,
   Or you shall pay for't. Don't be impertinent.   30
   None of your *freedoms*.

MESSENIO   By that single word
   I know I am a slave: 'tis briefly said,
   Plainly, and fully; yet I can't refrain
   From speaking. Mind me, Sir! Our purse, look here,   35
   'Tis light enough, 'twon't make us sweat; now verily,
   If you return not home, when nothing's left
   You'll sweat for this wild chase of your twin brother.
   As for the people here, these Epidamnians,
   They're errant debauchees, most potent drinkers;   40

---

12 The Istrians were a people of northern Italy; the Illyrians of southern Yugoslavia; the Massilians of
   southern France, or Marseilles.

26 A proverbial expression meaning you make a difficulty when there is none.

Cheats, parasites abound here; and they say
Such wheedling harlotries are no where met with.
For this the place is call'd Epidamnum,
Because there's no one comes here but says damn 'em.

M. SOSICLES I'll look to that; give me the purse. 45

MESSENIO The purse?
What would you do with it?

M. SOSICLES I've apprehensions
'Bout you, from what you said.

MESSENIO What apprehensions? 50

M. SOSICLES Lest you should cry in Epidamnum, damn 'em.
You are a mighty lover of the wenches:
I'm choleric, quite a madman when provok'd.
Now when I have the cash in my own hands,
'Twill guard against two harms: you'll not offend: 55
Nor I be angry with you.

MESSENIO Take and keep it—
With all my soul.

Scene 2

(*Enter* CYLINDRUS)

CYLINDRUS I've marketed most rarely, 60
And to my mind, I warrant, I'll serve up
A dainty dinner to the guests. But hold—
I see Menaechmus. Woe then to my back!
The guests are walking here before the door,
Ere I return from the market. I'll approach them. 65
Save you, Menaechmus!

M. SOSICLES Save you! Do you know me?

CYLINDRUS No, to be sure! (*ironically*) Where are the other guests?

M. SOSICLES What guests do you mean?

CYLINDRUS Your Parasite. 70

M. SOSICLES My Parasite?
Surely the man is mad.

MESSENIO Now say, my master,
Did I not tell you there were many cheats here?

M. SOSICLES Whom mean you by my Parasite? 75

CYLINDRUS Why, *Dishcloth*.

MESSENIO See, see—I have him safe here in the wallet.

CYLINDRUS Menaechmus, you are come too soon to dinner;
I am but now return'd from marketing.

M. SOSICLES What is the price, pray, of a hog for sacrifice? 80

CYLINDRUS One piece.

M. SOSICLES I'll give it; make a sacrifice
At my expense, for sure you must be mad
To cross a stranger thus, whoe'er you are.

CYLINDRUS I am Cylindrus; know you not my name? 85

M. SOSICLES Or Cylinder, or Cullender: begone.
I know you not, nor do I want to know you.
CYLINDRUS Your name's Menaechmus, that I know.
M. SOSICLES You talk
As one that's in his senses, calling me
Thus by my name. But where, pray, have you known me?
CYLINDRUS Where have I known you?—you, who have a wench here,
Erotium, my mistress?
M. SOSICLES I have not,
Nor know I who you are.
CYLINDRUS Not who I am?
I, who so oft have handed you the cup
When you carous'd here.
MESSENIO O that I have nothing
To break his head with!
M. SOSICLES How? you've handed me
The cup? when till this day I never came
To Epidamnum, never set my eyes on't.
CYLINDRUS Will you deny it?
M. SOSICLES Yes, I must deny it.
CYLINDRUS Don't you live yonder?
M. SOSICLES Plague upon their heads
That live there!
CYLINDRUS Sure he's mad, to curse himself.
Hark'ye, Menaechmus?
M. SOSICLES What say you?
CYLINDRUS If you would
Take my advice, that piece you promised me,
Buy a hog with it for yourself to sacrifice,*
For sure you are not in your perfect mind,
To curse yourself.
M. SOSICLES Thou'rt mad—vexatious fellow!
CYLINDRUS In this wise will he often jest with me;
He's such a wag, he—when his wife's not by.
M. SOSICLES Prithee now.
CYLINDRUS Prithee now, is this provision
Sufficient, what you see here, for you three?
Or would you have me to provide yet more
For you, your parasite, and wench?
M. SOSICLES What wench,
What parasite d'ye speak of?
MESSENIO Rascal! what
Provokes thee to molest him thus?
CYLINDRUS What business
Hast thou with me? I know thee not: I'm talking
To him I know.

90

95

100

105

110

115

120

125

130

---

114 Pigs were frequently sacrificed to household gods in behalf of people thought to be insane.

MESSENIO   You are not in your senses.

CYLINDRUS   I'll have these cooked directly, (*Pointing to the provisions*) no fear
Without delay. Would you ought further with me?

M. SOSICLES   Go hang yourself.   135

CYLINDRUS   Go you and seat yourself,
While to the violence of Vulcan's rage
I these expose. I'll in and let Erotium
Know you are here that she may fetch you in,
Rather than you should wander here out-of-doors. (CYLINDRUS *goes in*)   140

Scene 3

M. SOSICLES   So, is he gone? I find there is some truth
In what you told me.

MESSENIO   Do but mind. It seems
Some harlot dwells here; so this crackbrain said
Who went hence even now.   145

M. SOSICLES   But I do marvel
How he should know my name.

MESSENIO   I' faith, no wonder.
This is the way of courtezans: they send
Their lacqueys and their wenches to the port   150
To ask, if any foreign ship arrive,
Whose is it, what's its name? Then instantly
They set themselves to work and stick like glue.
If they can lure some gull to their embraces,
Anon they turn him out, undone and ruin'd.   155
Sure a pirate vessel lurks within this port,
Which we in my opinion should beware.

M. SOSICLES   You counsel right.

MESSENIO   It will be known at last
How right it is, if you as rightly follow it.   160

M. SOSICLES   Softly a while. The door creaks; let us see
Who's coming forth.

MESSENIO   Meanwhile I'll lay this down; (*Lays down his wallet on some oars*)
Pray keep it safe, ye water-treading oars.

Scene 4

(*Enter* EROTIUM, *speaking to her Servants within*)   165

EROTIUM   Leave the door thus: I would not have it shut.
Begone. Make ready; see that ev'ry thing
Be done that's wanting; lay the couches smooth;
Let the perfumes be set on fire. 'Tis neatness
Lures the fond lover's heart. A pretty prospect   170
Defeats the panting lover, wins for us.
But where, where is he, whom the cook inform'd me
Was at the door? O there he is, a gentleman

From whom I draw much service and much profit;
And therefore I'm content that he should hold,   175
As he deserves, the highest place with me.
I'll go and speak to him. My life! my soul!
I marvel you should stand here at the door
That's open to you more than is your own;
Your own it is. Sweet, ev'ry thing is ready   180
Which you desir'd: nothing to stay you, love.
The dinner which you order'd we have got.
Now, whensoe'er you please, you may sit down.

M. SOSICLES Whom does the woman speak to?

EROTIUM Why, to you.   185

M. SOSICLES What business have I ever had with you?
What business have I now?

EROTIUM 'Tis Venus' will
I should prefer you before all my lovers.
Nor on your part unmerited, for you,   190
You only with your gifts enrich me.

M.. SOSICLES Sure
This woman's either mad or drunk, Messenio,
Thus to accost a stranger so familiarly.

MESSENIO Such practices are common here, I told you.   195
These are but leaves; but if we tarry here
Three days, the trees themselves will tumble on you.
The courtezans here are all money-traps.
But suffer me to speak to her.—Hark ye, woman!
A word with you.   200

EROTIUM What is't?

MESSENIO Where did you know
This gentleman?

EROTIUM Where he has long known me:
In Epidamnum here.   205

MESSENIO In Epidamnum?
He never set his foot in't till to-day.

EROTIUM Ah! you are pleas'd to joke, my dear Menaechmus.
But prithee, sweet, come in; 'twere better for you.

M. SOSICLES 'Fore heav'n the woman calls me by my name.   210
I marvel what this means.

MESSENIO She smells the purse
Which you have there—

M. SOSICLES That's rightly put in mind.
Here, take it. I shall know now if her love's   215
To me, or to the purse.

EROTIUM Let's in to dinner.

M. SOSICLES 'Tis a kind invitation, and I thank you.

EROTIUM Why did you bid me then to get a dinner?

M. SOSICLES I bid you get a dinner!   220

EROTIUM Yes, most certainly,
    For you and for your parasite.

M. SOSICLES A plague!
    What parasite? Why sure the woman's crazy.

EROTIUM Peniculus.   225

M. SOSICLES Who's that Peniculus?

EROTIUM The parasite; in other words, the *Dishcloth*.

M. SOSICLES O, what they wipe their shoes with?

EROTIUM He, I say,
    Who came with you this morning, when you brought me   230
    The robe that you had stolen from your wife.

M. SOSICLES How say you? I present you with a robe,
    That I had stolen from my wife? Art mad?
    The woman, sure, walks like a gelding, sleeping.

EROTIUM Why are you pleas'd to use me for your sport?   235
    And why do you deny what you have done?

M. SOSICLES What is it I deny? What have I done?

EROTIUM Given me a robe belonging to your wife.

M. SOSICLES I still deny it. I never had a wife,
    Nor have I; neither have I set my foot   240
    Within your doors since I was born. I din'd
    On ship-board, thence came hither, and here met you.

EROTIUM Ah! woe is me! what ship is't you are talking of?

M. SOSICLES A wooden one, oft weather-beaten, oft
    Bethump'd with mallets, like a tailor's pin-cushion,   245
    Peg close to peg.

EROTIUM I' prithee, now have done
    With jesting thus and come along with me.

M. SOSICLES Some other man you mean, I know not whom,
    Not me.   250

EROTIUM What! don't I know thee? not Menaechmus,
    The son of Moschus, who were born, thou say'st,
    At Syracuse, in Sicily, where erst
    Reign'd king Agathocles, and after Pinthia,
    And next him Liparo, who by his death   255
    The kingdom left to Hiero, now king.

M. SOSICLES 'Faith what you say is true.

MESSENIO O Jupiter!
    Did she not come from th   : knows you?

M. SOSICLES I can hold out nc   260

MESSENIO Stay, Sir, stay;
    For if you cross her thresho ., you're undone.

M. SOSICLES Be quiet. All is well; I will assent
    To whatsoe'er she says, so I but get
    Good entertainment and a fair reception.   265
    (*To* EROTIUM) For some time wittingly I have oppos'd you,
    Fearing this fellow here, lest he should tell

My wife concerning all—the robe and dinner.
Now when you please, we'll enter.

EROTIUM   Then you do not   270
Stay for the parasite?

M. SOSICLES   I neither stay
Nor care a rush for him; nor would I have him
Be let in when he comes.

EROTIUM   With all my heart.   275
But do you know, sweet, what I'd have you do?

M. SOSICLES   Command me what you will.

EROTIUM   That robe you gave me
I'd have you carry it to the embroiderer's
To be made up anew with such additions   280
As I shall order.

M. SOSICLES   What you say is right:
So will it not be known; nor will my wife,
If she should see you with it in the street,
Recognize it.   285

EROTIUM   So, then by and by,
Sweet, you will take it with you when you go.

M. SOSICLES   I will.

EROTIUM   Let's in now.

M. SOSICLES   I'll attend you presently,   290
I would just speak a word with him. (EROTIUM *goes in*)

Scene 5

M. SOSICLES   Messenio!
Come here.

MESSENIO   What's the matter?

M. SOSICLES   Hm! shall I   295
Tell it to you?

MESSENIO   What?

M. SOSICLES   What a chance!

MESSENIO   What chance?

M. SOSICLES   I know what you will say.   300

MESSENIO   I say
So much the worse for you.

M. SOSICLES   I've got it, boy:
I have already made a rare beginning.
Quick as you can, go carry these my shipmates   305
Directly to some place for travelers.
Then come to me e'er sun-set.

MESSENIO   Master! master!
You're unacquainted with these harlotries.

M. SOSICLES   Peace, prithee. If I play the fool, 'tis I,   310
Not you, shall suffer. Why, this woman here

Is a mere simpleton, an arrant ignorant,
As far I have prov'd her hitherto.
She is our game, my boy.

MESSENIO 'Tis over with us.

M. SOSICLES Will you be gone?

MESSENIO He is undone, that's certain.
This pirate vessel has the boat in tow.
But I'm a fool that I should seek to rule
My master, for he bought me to obey,
Not govern him. Come, follow me, that I
May wait upon him at the time he order'd. (*Exeunt*)

Act Three

Scene 1

(*Enter* PENICULUS, *the Parasite*)

PENICULUS I have seen thirty years and more, yet never
Play'd I so foolish or so vile a trick
As I have done this day, in mixing with
The crowd in the assembly of the people.
Where while I stood staring about, Menaechmus
Gave me the slip, I fancy to his mistress—
Nor took me with him. Gods confound the man
First took it in his head to institute
These meetings to engage the most engag'd.
'Twere better only to convene the idle
Who should be fin'd in case of non-attendance.
There are enough who eat their meals alone,
Who've nought to do, who are not invited,
Nor e'er invite. These were the men to hold
Assemblies and attend at the Comitia;*
Had this been so, I had not lost my dinner,
Which he'd as sure have giv'n me, as I live.
I'll go however—Hope of the very scraps
Comforts my mind. But see, Menaechmus comes
From dinner with a wreath. All's ta'en away,
And I am come at a fine time indeed!

Scene 2

(*Enter* MENAECHMUS SOSICLES, *with a robe*)

M. SOSICLES If I return it neatly fitted up, (*Speaking to* EROTIUM *within*)
So that you scarce shall know it is the same,
And that this very day, shall you not then
Be satisfied?

---

[16] The Assembly at which the Romans elected officers or made laws.

PENICULUS (*Apart*) He's carrying the robe
To the embroiderer's—And dinner's done—
The wine drunk off, and the poor parasite bilk'd. 30
By Hercules! if I put up with this
And not revenge, I'm not the man I am.
Let's first see what he'll do and then accost him.

M. SOSICLES Immortal Gods! is there a man on whom
You've in one day bestow'd more good, or one 35
Who less could hope for it? I've din'd, I've drank,
I've feasted with my mistress, have born off
This robe, which she no more shall call her own.

PENICULUS (*Apart*) He speaks so softly, I can scarce distinguish
What 'tis he says: sure, now his belly's full, 40
He talks of me and of my share at dinner.

M. SOSICLES She told me I had given her the robe
And that I'd stol'n it from my wife; tho' I
Knew she was wrong, I seemingly assented
To all her story as if both of us 45
Had been joint parties in the whole transaction,
Said as she said. What need of many words?
I never in my life have far'd so well,
And at so small expense.

PENICULUS I will accost him. 50
I'm out of patience till I quarrel with him.

M. SOSICLES Who is this that is coming to accost me?

PENICULUS Tell me, inconstant, lighter than a feather,
Thou worst of men, most wicked of mankind,
Base man, deceiver, void of faith and honour! 55
Have I deserv'd this of thee? For what cause
Hast thou undone me? Say, have I deserv'd
That thou should'st steal thyself away from me,
Back at the Forum? And thou hast buried
The dinner in my absence, to the which 60
I was joint heir—how dare you serve me thus?

M. SOSICLES Prithee, young man, what hast to do with me?
Abusing thus a man thou dost not know,
For this you'll bring disaster on your head.

PENICULUS You have done that already. 65

M. SOSICLES Answer me.
Tell me your name, young man.

PENICULUS Still mocking me?
As if you did not know my name?

M. SOSICLES In troth, 70
I know not till this day I ever saw thee,
Nor art thou known to me. Who'er thou art,
It ill-becomes thee to be troublesome.

PENICULUS Not know me?

M. SOSICLES If I did, I'd not deny it.   75

PENICULUS Awake, Menaechmus.

M. SOSICLES 'Troth, I do not know
  That I'm asleep.

PENICULUS Not know your parasite?

M. SOSICLES Thy head is turn'd, young man, in my opinion.   80

PENICULUS Answer me, did you not this very day
  Steal from your wife that robe and give't Erotium?

M. SOSICLES I have no wife, nor have a robe stol'n,
  Nor given it to Erotium.

PENICULUS You're mad!   85
  Have you your senses? Why the thing's apparent!
  Did I not see you coming from the house,
  Carrying the robe?

M. SOSICLES Woe upon thy head!
  'Cause you're a rogue, think you we all are such?   90
  You say you saw me carrying this robe?

PENICULUS I did, by Hercules!

M. SOSICLES Go and be hang'd
  As you deserve, or else go purge your brain,
  For thou'rt the veriest madman I e'er met with.   95

PENICULUS By Pollux'* temple, nothing shall prevent me,
  From telling your wife everything that's pass'd.
  And then shall all this scurrile wit redound
  Back on yourself. Nor shall I forget
  You've swallow'd down my dinner.   100

M. SOSICLES What is this?
  Shall ev'ry one I see affront me thus?
  But see, the door is opening.

Scene 3

(*Enter a* MAID SERVANT *from the house of* EROTIUM, *with a clasp*)

SERVANT Erotium   105
  Most earnestly entreats of her Menaechmus,
  ('Twill make it but one trouble,) to bear *this*
  To the goldsmith, with her orders, that he add
  An ounce more gold and have it clean'd and mended.

M. SOSICLES This and ought else that she would have me do,   110
  Tell her I will take care to execute.

SERVANT But do you know the clasp I'm speaking of?

M. SOSICLES I know it not, but see 'tis made of gold.

SERVANT 'Tis that which sometimes since you said you stole,
  And privately, from your wife's chest of drawers.   115

M. SOSICLES That's what I never did, by Hercules!

SERVANT What, don't you recollect it? Then, return it.

---

[96] One of the twin sons of Zeus-Jupiter; Castor was his brother.

M. SOSICLES   Stay: I begin to recollect; it was
   The same I gave your mistress.
SERVANT   Yes, the same.   120
M. SOSICLES   Where are the bracelets which I gave with it?
SERVANT   You never gave them.
M. SOSICLES   But I did, by Pollux!
   And gave them both together.
SERVANT   Shall I say,   125
   You will take care—
M. SOSICLES   Yes, and the robe and clasp
   Shall be return'd together—
SERVANT   Let me, Sir,
   Beg you'd present me with a pair of earrings   130
   Of gold, and of two piece value, that I may
   Look well upon you when you pay your visits.
M. SOSICLES   It shall be done. Give me the gold; I'll pay
   Myself the fashion.
SERVANT   No, I pray you, Sir,   135
   Give it yourself, I'll be accountable.
M. SOSICLES   I say, give me the gold—
SERVANT   Another time.
   I'll pay it back two-fold.
M. SOSICLES   I have no money.   140
SERVANT   But when you have, you'll pay the jeweller.
   Any commands for me?
M. SOSICLES   Yes, tell your mistress
   I'll take great care of what she has order'd me—(*Exit Servant*)
   (*Aside*) Yes, soon as may be, I'll take care to sell them   145
   To the best bidder. Is she now gone in?
   She is, and shut the door. Sure all the gods
   Befriend me and heap favour upon favour.
   Why do I stay when time and opportunity
   Thus favours me in quitting this vile place.   150
   This place of bawds and panders?
   Haste thee, then Menaechmus; use well thy feet
   And mend thy pace. Let me take off my wreath
   And throw it to the left, so, if I'm follow'd,
   They may suppose I'm gone that way. I'll now   155
   Find, if I can, my servant and acquaint him
   With what the gods are doing in my favour. (*Exit*)

Act Four

Scene 1

(*Enter the* WIFE *of Menaechmus of Epidamnum and* PENICULUS, *the Parasite*)

WIFE   And shall I tamely then submit to live
In marriage with a man who filches from me
Whatever's in the house and bears it off
A present to his mistress?   5

PENICULUS   Hold your peace:
I will so order matters that you shall
Surprise him in the fact. So follow me.
Crown'd with a wreath and drunk, he bore away
The robe that he filch'd from you yesterday   10
To the embroiderer's. But see, the wreath,
The very wreath he wore—Is it not true? (*Seeing the wreath on the ground*)
He's gone this way, and you may trace his steps.
And see, by Pollux' temple, he returns,
And opportunely, but without the robe.   15

WIFE   How shall I treat him now?

PENICULUS   How? Why as usual,
Most heartily abuse him.

WIFE   Yes, I think so—

PENICULUS   Let's stand aside, and watch him from our ambush. (*They retire*)   20

Scene 2

(*Enter* MENAECHMUS EPIDAMNUM)

M. EPIDAMNUM   How troublesome it is thus to indulge
Ourselves in foolish customs! Yet the great
Of Rome are also guilty of it.
All wish to have a number of dependents,   25
But little care whether they're good or bad.
Their riches, not their qualities, they mind.
Honest and poor is bad. Wicked and rich
Are virtuous. Clients that have regard
To neither law nor common honesty   30
Have zealous patrons. Yet leave them a trust
They will deny it. The litigious,
Covetous, fraudulent, who've got their wealth
By usury or perjury—Their soul's
Still in litigation—They love the courts   35
And when they're called, their patrons must appear;
'Fore the people, praetor, commissary,
To speak in their behalf, however wrong.
Thus was I plagu'd today by a dependant,
One of this sort who would not let me do   40
Aught which I wanted in my own affairs.

Holding me close to his, he so detain'd me—
When I had battled for him 'fore the Aediles,*
With craft had pleaded his bad cause, had brought
To hard conditions his opponent, nay   45
Had more or less perplex'd the controversy
And brought it e'en to making their deposits—*
What does he do? He gave his bail and straightway
I never saw a villain more quickly proved
In all respects. Three witnesses swore plumb   50
And prov'd against him every accusation.
The gods confound him for thus making me
Lose all my time; ay, and confound myself
For having seen the Forum with these eyes!
The noblest day is lost: a dinner's order'd;   55
My mistress waits. I knew it, and as soon
As e'er I could I've hast'ned from the Forum.
Doubtless she's angry with me; but the robe
Filch'd from my wife today and sent to her
Shall make all up.   60

PENICULUS   What say you now?

WIFE   Unhappy!
In having such a husband.

PENICULUS   Did you hear
Distinctly what he said?   65

WIFE   Very distinctly.

M. EPIDAMNUM   I shall do right if I go in directly
And here refresh myself.

WIFE   Wait but a little,
And I'll refresh you better. (*To him*) You shall pay,   70
Yes, and that you shall, by Castor! and with interest,
For what you filch'd from me. Now take your due.
What, did you fancy you could play such tricks
In secret?

M. EPIDAMNUM   What's the business, wife?   75

WIFE   Ask that
Of me?

M. EPIDAMNUM   Why, would you that I ask of him?

PENICULUS   No soothing now. Go on.

M. EPIDAMNUM   Say, why so pensive?   80

WIFE   You can't but know the reason—

PENICULUS   Yes, he knows,
But cunningly dissembles.

M. EPIDAMNUM   What's the matter?

WIFE   The robe.—   85

M. EPIDAMNUM   The robe? what—

[43] Officials in charge of public works.
[47] This probably means the litigants made deposits assuring that they would stand trial, thus gaining time.

WIFE Ay, the robe.—

PENICULUS Why pale?

M. EPIDAMNUM I pale! unless the paleness of the robe
    Has made me so.   90

PENICULUS I too am pale, because
    You ate the supper and thought not of me.
    (*To the wife*) To him again.

M. EPIDAMNUM Won't you be silent?

PENICULUS No.   95
    (*To the wife*) He nods to me to hold my tongue.

M. EPIDAMNUM Not I,
    By Hercules! I neither wink'd nor nodded.

WIFE I'm an unhappy woman!

M. EPIDAMNUM Why unhappy?   100
    Explain—

PENICULUS A rare assurance, that denies
    What yourself sees.

M. EPIDAMNUM By Jove and all the gods!
    I nodded not. Are you now satisfied?   105

PENICULUS And to be sure, she now will give you credit.
    Go back again—

M. EPIDAMNUM And whither?

PENICULUS Whither else
    But to th' embroiderer. Beyond all doubt   110
    I think you ought. Go, and bring back the robe—

M. EPIDAMNUM What robe do you speak of?

WIFE Since he don't remember
    What he has done, I have no more to say.

M. EPIDAMNUM Has any of the servants been in fault?   115
    Has any of the men or women slaves
    Given you a saucy answer? Say, speak out;
    He shall not go unpunish'd.

WIFE Sure, you trifle.

M. EPIDAMNUM You're out of humour: that   120
    I'm not quite pleas'd with.

WIFE You trifle still.

M. EPIDAMNUM Has any of the family
    Done ought to make you angry?

WIFE Trifling still.   125

M. EPIDAMNUM Angry with me then—

WIFE Now you trifle not.

M. EPIDAMNUM 'Troth, I've done nothing to deserve it of you.

WIFE Trifling again.

M. EPIDAMNUM What is it gives you pain?   130
    Tell me, my dear.

PENICULUS He sooths you. Civil creature!

M. EPIDAMNUM (*To Peniculus*) Can't you be quiet? I don't speak to you.

WIFE Off with your hand.

PENICULUS (*Aside*) Ay, thus you're rightly serv'd—
  Dine then again in haste when I am absent
  And rally me before the house when drunk!
  A wreath, too, on your head!

M. EPIDAMNUM By Pollux' temple!
  I have not din'd to-day, nor have I once
  Set foot within the house.

PENICULUS You dare deny it?

M. EPIDAMNUM I do, by Hercules!

PENICULUS Consummate impudence!
  Did I not see you with a wreath of flowers,
  Standing before the house here—when you said
  My head was turn'd, when you denied you knew me,
  And when you'd pass upon me for a stranger?

M. EPIDAMNUM I do assure you since I slip'd away
  This morning from you I've not been till now
  At home.

PENICULUS I know you, Sir: but you knew not
  I'd wherewithal to take revenge upon you.
  I've told your wife the whole, by Hercules!

M. EPIDAMNUM What have you told?

PENICULUS I know not. Ask of her.

M. EPIDAMNUM What's this, my dear? What is it he has told you?
  You answer not. Why don't you say what 'tis?

WIFE As if you know not. Why, a robe has been
  Stol'n from me, in my house.

M. EPIDAMNUM A robe stol'n from you?

WIFE Do you ask me?

M. EPIDAMNUM In troth, I scarce should ask it,
  Was I assur'd it was so.

PENICULUS Wicked man!
  How he dissembles! But you can't conceal it,
  I know the whole affair; and I have told it
  All to your wife.

M. EPIDAMNUM What is all this about?

WIFE Since you have lost all shame, and won't confess
  The thing yourself, hearken to me and hear it:
  I'll tell you what has made me out of humour
  And everything now discover'd to me.
  You have done well for *me,* stealing my robe.

M. EPIDAMNUM Done well for *you* by stealing of your robe!

PENICULUS Observe his subterfuge. 'Twas stol'n for her (*Meaning* EROTIUM)
  And not for *you.* Had it been stol'n for *you,*
  It had been safe.

M. EPIDAMNUM I've nought to do with you.
  (*To his wife*) But what say you?

WIFE I say, I've lost from home
  A robe.

M. EPIDAMNUM Who took it?

WIFE He who stole it knows.

M. EPIDAMNUM And who is he?   185

WIFE One who is call'd Menaechmus.

M. EPIDAMNUM Spitefully done! And who is this Menaechmus?

WIFE Yourself, I hear.

M. EPIDAMNUM What! I?

WIFE Yes, you.   190

M. EPIDAMNUM Who said so?

WIFE My self.

PENICULUS And I; and that you had carried it
  Off to your mistress, to Erotium.

M. EPIDAMNUM I?   195
  I give it her?

PENICULUS You, you, I say. Shall I
  Go fetch an owl, to hoot in at your ears ,
  You. You? For we are both quite tir'd

M. EPIDAMNUM By Jove and all the gods, I swear, my dear,   200
  I never gave it her. Will that content you?

PENICULUS And I, I swear, by Hercules! that we
  Say nought but truth.

M. EPIDAMNUM I did not give it to her,
  I only lent it.   205

WIFE 'Troth, I never lend
  Your coat nor cloak abroad. 'Tis right for women
  To lend out women's clothes, and men, their own.
  Won't you return my robe?

M. EPIDAMNUM The robe, I'll see   210
  Shall be return'd—

WIFE 'Tis the best way. For you
  Shall never set a foot within your doors,
  Unless you bring my robe.

M. EPIDAMNUM Not set a foot   215
  Within my doors?

PENICULUS (*To the Wife*) What recompense for me,
  Who have assisted you?

WIFE When you have had
  A loss like mine, I'll do the same for you   220

PENICULUS By Pollux' temple! that will never be,
  For I have nought at home to lose. The gods
  Confound you both, both of you, wife and husband!
  I'll hie me to the Forum, for I find
  'Tis now quite over with me in this family.   225

          (*Exeunt* PENICULUS *and the* WIFE, *severally*)

M. EPIDAMNUM My wife then thought she'd done a mighty matter

In threatening thus to shut me out of doors,
As if I had not a far better place
Where I shall be admitted. Well, if I   230
Displease you, my dear wife, I must e'en bear it;
But I shall please Erotium, and she ne'er
Will shut me out, but rather shut me in.
Well, I'll go in, and pray her to return
The robe I just now gave her, and instead   235
Of that, I'll purchase her a better. Ho!
Who's porter here? Open the door and call
Erotium hither.

Scene 3

(*Enter* EROTIUM)

EROTIUM   Who inquires for me?   240

M. EPIDAMNUM   'Tis one who to himself is more enemy
Than such to you.

EROTIUM   My dear Menaechmus
Do'st stand before the door? Follow me in.

M. EPIDAMNUM   Stay here a little. Do you know the reason   245
I now come to you?

EROTIUM   I know it very well:
'Tis to amuse and please yourself with me.

M. EPIDAMNUM   That robe I lately gave you, prithee, love,
Restore it, for my wife hath been appris'd   250
And knows the whole affair from first to last.
I'll buy one for you twice as rich; you'll like—

EROTIUM   I gave it you but now, to carry it
To th' embroiderer's, and with it a bracelet
To give the jeweller to set a-new.   255

M. EPIDAMNUM   You gave to me a bracelet, and the robe?
Never. For when I'd giv'n the robe to you
I went directly to the market-place.
Now first return I; nor have seen you since.

EROTIUM   I see through your design: because I trusted you,   260
You would deceive me. What a way to act!

M. EPIDAMNUM   I do not ask you for it to defraud you,
But tell you that my wife knows all the affair.

EROTIUM   Nor did I ask you for it; you yourself
Gave it me freely; as a gift, you gave it.   265
And now you ask it back. Well, be it so:
Let it be yours; take it; make use of it—
You or your wife—preserve it as your eyes.
But don't deceive yourself; after this day
You never shall set foor within my doors,   270
Since you have treated with contempt a woman

Who has not merited such usage from you.
Next time you come, be sure bring money with you
You shall not have to visit me for nothing.
Henceforth find some one else to disappoint. 275

M. EPIDAMNUM   You are too hasty—Hark you!—Stay—Come back.

EROTIUM   Still are you there? and dare on my account
Still to return? (*Exit* EROTIUM)

M. EPIDAMNUM   She's gone— has shut the door.
Now I'm turn'd out indeed; nor can I gain 280
Credit or from my mistress or my wife.
I'll go, consult my friends in the affair.

Scene 4

(*Enter* MENAECHMUS SOSICLES, *with the robe*)

M. SOSICLES   'Twas foolish in me when but now I trusted
My purse with all that's in it to Messenio. 285
He has got, I doubt, into some brothel with it.

(*Enter the* WIFE *of Menaechmus of Epidamnum*)

WIFE   I'll now see if my husband is come home.
But see, he's here! All's well, he brings my robe.

M. SOSICLES   I wonder where Messenio can be got! 290

WIFE   I'll go and talk to him as he deserves.
Art not asham'd, vile man, to appear before me,
And with this robe?

M. SOSICLES   Why, what's the matter, woman?
What is't disturbs you! 295

WIFE   Dare you, impudence!
Mutter a single word, or speak to me?

M. SOSICLES   What have I done I should not dare speak?

WIFE   What! Do you ask me? O, consummate inpudence!

M. SOSICLES   Did you ne'er hear, good woman, why the Grecians 300
Call'd Hecuba a bitch?

WIFE   Not that I know of.

M. SOSICLES   Because she did the same that you do now;
Threw out abuse on every one she saw:
And therefore, rightly did they call her bitch. 305

WIFE   I cannot bear these scandalous reproaches:
I'd rather be a widow all my life
Than bear these vile reflections you throw on me.

M. SOSICLES   What is't to me whether you live as married
Or parted from your husband? Is it thus 310
The custom to sing out such idle stories
To strangers on their first arrival here?

WIFE   What idle stories? No, I will not bear it,
I'd rather live a widow than endure
Your humours any longer. 315

M. SOSICLES 'Troth, for me
　　Long as you please you've leave to live a widow:
　　As long as Jupiter shall keep his kingdom.
WIFE You would not own but now you stole that robe,
　　And now you hold it out before my eyes?　　　　　320
　　What, are you not asham'd?
M. SOSICLES By Hercules!
　　You are an impudent and wicked woman
　　To dare to say this robe was stol'n from you
　　When it was given me by another woman,　　　　325
　　To get it alter'd for her.
WIFE Yes, by Castor!
　　I'll call my father hither and lay open
　　All your base actions to him. (*To a Servant*) Decius, go,
　　Seek for my father, bring him with you; say　　　330
　　'Tis proper he should come. I'll tell him all
　　Your horrid usage.
M. SOSICLES Are you in your senses?
　　What horrid usage?
WIFE How you have filch'd from me　　　　335
　　My robe, my gold, from me who are your wife,
　　And giv'n them to your mistress. Is not that
　　The very truth?
M. SOSICLES I prithee, woman, say
　　Where I may sup, to save me from your tongue.　　340
　　I know not whom you take me for— For you,
　　I know as much of Parthaon.*
WIFE Tho' you mock me,
　　You can't, by Pollux! serve my father so,
　　Who's just now coming hither. Look behind.　　345
　　Say, do you know him?
M. SOSICLES Just as I know Calchas.*
　　The very day that I saw you, I say,
　　This day did I see him—
WIFE Dar'st thou deny　　　　350
　　That thou know'st me, deny thou know'st my father?
M. SOSICLES I'd say that the same thing did'st thou bring thy grandfather.
WIFE By Castor! you are like yourself in all things.

Scene 5

(*Enter* OLD MAN)

OLD MAN Fast as my age permits and the occasion　　355
　　Calls will I push my steps and hasten forward.
　　How easily, I easily may guess.

---

342 Father of Eneus, grandfather of Deianira, Hercules' wife. Used here because he lived a long time before.
347 The soothsayer for the Greeks at Troy.

My speed forsakes me; I'm beset with age;
I bear a weak, yet heavy laden body.
Old age is a sad pedlar, on his back   360
Carrying a full pack of grievances;
It would be tedious to recount them all.
But this affair I cannot well digest.
What should this matter be which makes my daughter
Want me to come to her in such a hurry?   365
She does not tell me what the business is,
What 'tis she wants, nor why she sends for me;
Yet I can give a shrewd guess what it is:
I'm apt to think some quarrel with her husband.
Such is their way, who of their portions proud   370
Would keep their husbands under government.
Nor are the husbands often without fault.
But there are bounds how far a wife should go.
Nor does my daughter send to see her father,
But only when some fault's committed, or   375
Some quarrel has arisen. What it is,
I soon shall know, for, look, I see her there
Before the door, and with her, too, her husband,
Whose looks are pensive. 'Tis as I suspected.
I'll call her.   380

WIFE   I'll go meet him. Happiness
Attend you, father!

OLD MAN   That good will to you!
Am I come to see things go on well?
Wherefore your order that I should be sent for?   385
Why are you pensive, say? and what's the reason
Your husband keeps aloof in anger from you?
The reason, come now; sure there has been
Some bickering between you. Who's in fault?
Tell in few words—no long discourse about it.   390

WIFE   I am in nought to blame, be easy then
As to that point, my father. But I cannot
Live longer with him, nor stay longer here.
Therefore, I beg you, take me hence away.

OLD MAN   Say, what's the matter?   395

WIFE   Matter? I am made
A laughing-stock.

OLD MAN   By whom?

WIFE   By him you've made
My husband.   400

OLD MAN   So! A quarrel! Say, how often
I've warn'd you both not to complain to me?

WIFE   How can I help it, Sir?

OLD MAN What! Ask you me?

WIFE Yes, if you'll give me leave.

OLD MAN How many times
    Have I advis'd you to conform to your husband?
    Never to watch his actions, where he goes,
    Or what he is about.

WIFE But he's in love,
    Here in the neighbourhood, with a courtezan.

OLD MAN He's wise in that; and by that care of yours,
    In thus observing him, I would advise him
    To love still more.

WIFE He drinks there, too.

OLD MAN Think you
    You will make him drink the less, or there,
    Or elsewhere, as he likes? What impudence!
    Do you insist he never sup abroad,
    Nor entertain a stranger at your house?
    Would you your husband should obey your pleasure?
    You may as well require him to partake
    Your work with you, and sit among the maids,
    And card the wool.

WIFE I find, Sir, I have brought you
    No advocate for me, but for my husband.
    Here you stand as a patron in my cause,
    Yet plead for his.

OLD MAN Was he in ought to blame
    I should condemn him more than I do you.
    But when I see he keeps you richly cloth'd,
    Allows you servants, and a plenteous table,
    A wife thus treated, should in my opinion
    Bear towards him a more equal mind.

WIFE But he
    Pilfers my gold, my robe from out my chest,
    Robs me, and carries to his courtezans
    My richest ornaments.

OLD MAN If he acts thus,
    He acts amiss: if not, you act but ill
    When you accuse one that is innocent.

WIFE Why, even at this very instant,
    He has a bracelet and a robe of mine
    Which he bore off here to this courtezan;
    And now that I know it, he brings them back.

OLD MAN 'Tis right to know these matters from himself.
    I will accost, and speak to him. Say, Menaechmus,
    What's your dispute? Give me at once to know it.
    Why are you pensive? And why is your wife

405

410

415

420

425

430

435

440

445

In wrath against you? 450

M. SOSICLES Whoso'er you are .
Whate'er's your name, I call great Jupiter,
And all the gods to witness—

OLD MAN Why and wherefore?

M. SOSICLES That I this woman ne'er have injur'd her. 455
Who raves about my stealing from her house
This robe and bearing of it off. If ever
I've once set foot within her doors, I wish
I may become the veriest wretch alive.

OLD MAN Have you your senses when you make that wish, 460
Or when deny that ever you set foot
Within that house where you reside yourself?
O, of all madmen the most mad!

M. SOSICLES Old man,
And do you say, that I inhabit here? 465

OLD MAN Do you deny it?

M. SOSICLES By Hercules, I do!

WIFE 'Tis impudence to do so. But you mean
Because you went this night elsewhere.

OLD MAN Come hither, 470
Daughter—And you, (*to him*) what say you now?
This night went you from hence?

M. SOSICLES Whither? for what, I pray you?

OLD MAN I know not, I.

WIFE 'Tis plain he banters you. 475

OLD MAN (*To her*) What, can'st not hold thy tongue? Truly Menaechmus,
You've jested long enough: now to the purpose.

M. SOSICLES Pray, what have you to do with me? What business?
Say whence you come, and who you are, and what
I've done to you, or to this woman here, 480
That ye thus tease me?

WIFE How his eyes shine! See!
A greenish colour spreads o'er all his temples,
O'er all his forehead. See his eyes! they sparkle!

M. SOSICLES (*Aside*) Since they have me mad, what can I do? 485
Better then feign a madness, I may thus
Fright them away.

WIFE Look how he yawns and stretches!
What shall I do, my father!

OLD MAN Come this way, 490
As far off from him as you can, my child.

M. SOSICLES Evoï, Evoï!* Bacchus, son of Jove,
Why dost thou call me to the wood to hunt?
I hear you, but I cannot stir from hence.
This woman on the left side watches me 495

492 The cry of the frenzied followers of Dionysus-Bacchus.

32 PLAUTUS

Like a mad dog; on t'other, this old goat,
Who often in his life has by false witness
Destroy'd the guiltless man.

OLD MAN   Woe on thy life!

M. SOSICLES   See where Apollo from his oracle   500
Commands me to burn out both that woman's eyes,
With lighted torches.

WIFE   I'm undone, my father!
He threatens me, to burn out both my eyes.

M. SOSICLES (*Aside*):   Alas! they say I'm mad. They themselves   505
Are much more mad than I.

OLD MAN   Hark, you! Daughter!

WIFE   Your pleasure, Sir? What shall we do?

OLD MAN   Suppose
I call my servants quickly. I'll bring some who   510
Shall carry him into the house and bind him,
'Ere he make more disturbance.

M. SOSICLES (*Aside*)   On my word,
Unless I take great care, they'll bear me off
By force into their house. (*Aloud*) Yes, thou hast order'd me   515
Not to forbear the thrusting of my fists
Into her face, unless she marches off
Far from my sight and goes and hangs herself.
Yes, yes, Apollo, I obey thy orders.

OLD MAN   Run home, my daughter, run into the house   520
Fast as you can, lest he belabour you.

WIFE   I fly, I pray you take good heed, my father
That he escape not. An unhappy wife
Am I to hear all this. (*Exit*)

M. SOSICLES (*Aside*)   I've sent her off.   525
Not bad. And now must I send after her
This more than filthy fellow, this old grey beard,
This totterer, this old Tithon, son of Cygnus—*
(*Aloud*) 'Tis thy command that I should break his limbs,
His bones, his joints, with that same staff he carries.   530

OLD MAN   Touch or come nearer me and you'll repent it.

M. SOSICLES   Yes, I will do as you have order'd me,
Take up this two-edg'd axe, bone this old fellow,
And cut his bowels piece-meal.

OLD MAN   'Troth, I must   535
Take some care of myself. I am afraid,
He'll do a mischief to me, as he threatens.

M. SOSICLES   Apollo! Fast thou pour'st thy great behests.
Now thou command'st me harness my wild steeds,

---

528 Tithonus was the son of Laomedon, not of Cygnus. Beloved of Aurora, he was taken up to the heavens
where he enjoyed an immortality which, unfortunately, did not prevent him from aging. Menaechmus'
error is probably deliberate to support his madness.

Fierce and untam'd, and now to mount my car 540
And crush in pieces this Getulian lion,*
This stinking, toothless beast. Now do I mount,
And now I shake the reins—I take the lash;
Now fly, my steeds, and let your sounding hoofs
Tell your swift course. Show in the turn your speed. 545

OLD MAN And dost thou threaten me with harness'd steeds?

M. SOSICLES Again, Apollo! Thou again command'st me
To rush upon yon fellow that stands there
And murder him. But who is this that by
My fluttering tresses plucks me from my car, 550
The dire commands revoking of Apollo?

OLD MAN A sharp and obstinate distemper this!
Ye gods! is't possible, a man who seem'd
So well but now should fall so suddenly
Into so strange a malady? Away, 555
I must make haste and send for a physician. (*Exit*)

M. SOSICLES What, are they gone? Are they both fled my sight?
Who forc'd me in my wits to feign the madman.
What hinders now to 'mbark me, while I'm well?
I beg you, Sirs, (*to the spectators*) if the old man return, 560
Not to tell him what street I went down. (*Exit*)

Act Five

Scene 1

(*Enter* OLD MAN)

OLD MAN My limbs with sitting ache, my eyes with watering,
While this same doctor from his patients comes.
Scarcely arrived at home, he's telling me,
He was oblig'd to set a broken leg 5
Of Asclepius, and Apollo's arm.*
I'm thinking whether I am bringing with me,
Or a physician, or a carpenter.
But see! he comes, tho' at an ant's pace.

Scene 2

(*Enter* PHYSICIAN) 10

PHYSICIAN What did you say was his disorder, Sir?
Inform me, is he mad or is he frantic?
Is it a lethargy, or is he dropsical?

OLD MAN I brought you hither to know that of you,

---

541 Getulia was in Africa and was noted for its large, fierce lions.

6 The guardian divinities of medicine. For all the Old Man knows the doctor may, like a carpenter, have been repairing their statues.

So that your art should cure him.

PHYSICIAN   Nought more easy.
From this time I engage he shall be well.

OLD MAN   I'd have great care taken in his cure.

PHYSICIAN   My frequent visits will wear me out,
Such great care I shall take in curing him.   20

OLD MAN   But see the man!

PHYSICIAN   Let us observe his actions.

Scene 3

(*Enter* MENAECHMUS EPIDAMNUM)

M. EPIDAMNUM   This day has been unlucky, even to me
Quite adverse. What I thought to have done in secret   25
Has been discover'd by this Parasite
And brought both fear and infamy upon me.
He my Ulysses was and my adviser,
Yet nought but evil heaps on me his king.
His thread of life, if I but live myself,   30
I will cut off. How like a fool I talk!
His thread of life! His thread of life is mine:
He eats my victuals, lives at my expense.
Yes, I will be the death of him, Besides,
This wench has acted but in character—   35
The manner of them all. When I request her
To give me back the robe to give my wife,
She tells me she already had return'd it.
'Troth, I'm unhappy!

OLD MAN   Hear you what he says?   40

PHYSICIAN   He says he is unhappy.

OLD MAN   Pray go nearer.

PHYSICIAN   Save you, Menaechmus. Why do you bare your arms?
You know not how it works on your disorder.

M. EPIDAMNUM   Go, hang yourself.   45

PHYSICIAN   What think you now?

M. EPIDAMNUM   What think?
What can I think?

PHYSICIAN   To work a cure requires
More than an acre of good hellebore.   50
Hark ye! Menaechmus?

M. EPIDAMNUM   What would'st thou with me?

PHYSICIAN   Answer to what I ask. Say, do you drink
White wine or red?

M. EPIDAMNUM   Go, hang yourself.   55

PHYSICIAN   I find
The mad fit just now coming on.

M. EPIDAMNUM   Why not

Ask me as well the colour of my bread,
Whether I eat it purple, red, or yellow?   60
Whether eat scaly birds, or feather'd fish.

OLD MAN   Hark! how deliriously he talks! Before
He grows stark staring mad, give him some potion.

PHYSICIAN   Hold, stay a little, I shall further question him.

OLD MAN   More idle talk will quite demolish him.   65

PHYSICIAN   Tell me but this. Do you ever find your eyes
Grow hard?

M. EPIDAMNUM   Do you take me for a locust, fool?

PHYSICIAN   Do you find your bowels make a noise sometimes?

M. EPIDAMNUM   When I am full, my bowels make no noise;   70
They do, when I am hungry.

PHYSICIAN   By my troth,
In this he does not answer like a madman.
D'you sleep till day-light? When you go to bed,
D'you get to sleep with ease?   75

M. EPIDAMNUM   My debts discharg'd.
I sleep with ease. May Jove and all the gods
Confound this questioner!

PHYSICIAN (*Aside*)   He 'gins to rave.
Take heed of what you say.   80

OLD MAN   In what he says,
He's much more moderate than he was but now.
'Tis but a while ago he said his wife
Was a mad bitch.

M. EPIDAMNUM   What did I say?   85

OLD MAN   You're mad,
I say.

M. EPIDAMNUM   What, I?

OLD MAN   You there, who threaten'd me,
You'd trample me beneath your horse's feet.   90
I heard you do it, and I will maintain it.

M. EPIDAMNUM   And I will know, you've stol'n Jove's sacred crown,
And for that have been confin'd in prison.
And when releas'd, you've been severely whip'd
Under a gibbet. And I know besides,   95
You've kill'd your father, and have sold your mother.
Think you I am so mad, I can't devise
The same abusive language against you,
As you can do 'gainst me?

OLD MAN   Doctor, I beg you,   100
What you intend to do to him, do quickly.
Do you not see he's mad?

PHYSICIAN   'Twere the best thing,
You know, to have him carried to my house.

OLD MAN   Do you think so?   105

PHYSICIAN   Why not? I there can treat him
　　As I think proper.
OLD MAN   Do just as you please.
PHYSICIAN   For about twenty days you shall drink hellebore.
M. EPIDAMNUM   And you, some thirty days, shall be tied up　　　110
　　And flog'd severely.
PHYSICIAN   Go and call your men
　　To bring him to my house.
OLD MAN   How many men
　　D'ye think will be sufficient?　　　115
PHYSICIAN   As I see him,
　　So mad, not less than four.
OLD MAN   They shall be here
　　Immediately. Take care of him, good doctor.
PHYSICIAN   I'll home to get things ready that are wanting.　　　120
　　Go, bid your servants bring him to my house.
OLD MAN   I will take care that he shall soon be there.
PHYSICIAN   I'm gone.
OLD MAN   Farewell. (*Exeunt* PHYSICIAN *and* OLD MAN *separately*)
M. EPIDAMNUM   The father-in-law is gone　　　125
　　And so's the doctor. Now I am alone.
　　How is it, Jove, these men will have me mad!
　　Since I was born, I've ne'er been sick one day.
　　Nor am I mad, nor do I seek for quarrels,
　　Nor stir up strifes. I'm well in health and see　　　130
　　Others the same. I know men, and speak to them.
　　Is't not that those who say that I am mad
　　Are mad themselves? What shall I do? I would
　　Go home; but then my wife will not permit it.
　　My mistress too will not admit me. Thus　　　135
　　All of it's ill. I'll e'en stay here till night,
　　Perhaps I'll get admittance in the dark. (*Stands apart*)

Scene 4

(*Enter* MESSENIO)

MESSENIO   'Tis on all hands allow'd to be the proof
　　Of a good servant when he takes good care of,　　　140
　　Looks after, thinks of, and disposes rightly
　　His master's business. That, when he is absent,
　　Things may go on as well, or even better,
　　Than when he's present. He whose heart is right
　　Will think his back of greater consequence　　　145
　　Than is his gullet; ay, and to his belly
　　Prefer his legs. He ought to bear in mind
　　The wages that servants good for nothing,
　　Or wicked, from their master's hands receive:

And these are, stripes and chains, the stocks, the mill,   150
Hard labour, cold and hunger. Such as these
Are the rewards of idleness. This evil
I'm terribly afraid of; thus I choose
Rather to do my duty than neglect it.
Words I can bear, but stripes I hate. I rather   155
Like to eat that which has been ground by others,
Than grind myself what others are to eat.
I therefore execute my master's orders
Well; and with sober diligence I serve him
This turns to my account. Let others act then   160
As best they think it for their interest,
I'll ever be that which I ought to be.
This fear I'll still retain, to keep me free
From fault; that wheresoe'er my master is,
I may be ready there to wait on him.   165
Those servants who have nothing done amiss,
Yet keep this fear, still make themselves of use
To their respective masters. But the servants
Who never live in fear of doing wrong,
Fear when they've something done to merit punishment.   170
As for myself, I shan't live long in fear.
The time draws nigh, when master will reward me
For all the pains I have been at to serve him.
I've serv'd him so as to preserve my back.
Now that I've plac'd the servants, as he order'd,   175
And what they'd want i'th'inn. I'm come to meet him.
I'll now knock at the door that he may know
I'm here, tho' doubtful whether I can bring him
Safe off from this vile house. I fear me much
Lest I come too late after the battle.   180

Scene 5

(*Enter* OLD MAN, *with Servants*)

OLD MAN (*To the Servants*) By gods and men, I here conjure you all
To take good care to execute the orders
Given you already, and I now repeat them.
See that man carried to the doctor's house;   185
On pain of both your sides and legs, obey me.
Be sure, each of you, not to heed his threats there.
Why stand you thus? why hesitate? E'en now
He ought to've been borne off. I'll go myself
Straight to the doctor. When you are got thither,   190
You'll find me there before you.(*Exit*)

M. EPIDAMNUM I'm undone.
What is the matter? What do these men want,

That they run here so fast? What is't you want?
Why do you thus surround me? Why thus hale me?   195
Where would you carry me? Undone! help! help!
Aid me, ye Epidamnians! (*To the Servants*) Let me go!

MESSENIO Ye gods, what do I see! What men are these
Who thus unworthily are bearing off
My master?   200

M. EPIDAMNUM What, will no one dare to help me?

MESSENIO Master, I will, and boldly too. What villainy!
Ye Epidamnians, thus to seize my master,
In the open street, by day-light, undisturb'd
By tumults in your city. A free man   205
He enter'd it. Then let him go, I say.

M. EPIDAMNUM Who'er you are, assist me, I beseech you,
Nor let them do such signal outrage on me.

MESSENIO Yes, I'll assist, defend, and succour you.
'Tis far more just that I myself should perish   210
Than suffer you to be thus treated, master.
Pluck out that fellow's eye, I beg of you,
Who holds you by the shoulder. I'll myself
Plant in these rascal chaps a crop of blows.
If you persist in bearing him away,   215
You'll find you'll have the worst of it. Let him go.

M. EPIDAMNUM I've got hold of the rascal's eye.

MESSENIO Why then, scratch!
Rogues! Rascals!

SERVANTS You'll murder us. Have mercy!   220

MESSENIO Let him go, then.

M. EPIDAMNUM What is't ye mean, you rascals!
By laying hands on me thus violently?
Curry the scoundrels with your blows.

MESSENIO Away,   225
Begone, go and be hang'd, ye rascals!
You there, that are the last to quit your hold,
Take this along with you as a reward. (*Strikes him*)
So, so: I think I've on this scoundrel's chaps
Written in red letters. 'Troth, I came in time   230
To your assistance, master.

M. EPIDAMNUM May the gods,
Whoe'er you are, be ever kind to you
Young man. For without you I ne'er had seen
The setting sun this day.   235

MESSENIO By Pollux! therefore,
If you do right, you'll give me, Sir, my freedom.

M. EPIDAMNUM Give you your freedom!

MESSENIO Out of doubt, my master,
Since I have sav'd your life.   240

M. EPIDAMNUM How's this! young man,
You are mistaken.

MESSENIO I mistaken! how?

M. EPIDAMNUM I swear by father Jupiter, I'm not
Your master.   245

MESSENIO Can you say so?

M. EPIDAMNUM I don't lie.
I never had a servant yet; I say,
Who ever did for me, what you have done?

MESSENIO If then you will not own me for your servant,   250
E'en let me go and have my liberty.

M. EPIDAMNUM As far as in my power, take your liberty,
And go where'er you please.

MESSENIO Then you command me?

M. EPIDAMNUM Indeed, as far as I've a right to do so.   255

MESSENIO My patron, thanks!

A SERVANT I joy to see you free, Messenio.

MESSENIO In troth I well believe you.
By Hercules! I do. And now, my patron,
I beg you'd lay on me the same commands   260
As when I was your servant. I'll live with you;
And, when you home return, go with you, Sir.

M. EPIDAMNUM No, by no means.

MESSENIO I'll go now to the inn
And bring your goods and money to you straight.   265
The purse which has your money is fast seal'd
Within the cloak-bag. I'll go bring it straight.

M. EPIDAMNUM Do so, and quickly.

MESSENIO Sir, I'll bring them back
In the same state as when you gave them me.   270
Wait for me here. (*Exit*)

M. EPIDAMNUM What I've to-day experienc'd
Of all days is most extraordinary.
Some of them say that I am not the man
I am and shut me out of doors. And here   275
A man insists he is my servant—
And I just now have given him his freedom.
He talks of bringing money to me straight,
Which if he does, I'll tell him he has liberty
To go from me whene'er it suits him best.   280
My father-in-law and the physician say
That I am mad. 'Tis strange what this should be:
It seems to me no other than a dream.
I'll now go to this courtezan and see,
Tho' she is angry with me, if I can't   285
Prevail on her, to let me have the robe
To carry home and return to my wife. (*Exit*)

Scene 6

(Enter MENAECHMUS SOSICLES *and* MESSENIO*)*

M. SOSICLES   And do you dare affirm, audacious fellow,
That you have met me any where today,   290
When I had order'd you to meet me here?

MESSENIO   It is so true that I not only met you,
But that e'en now I freed you from four men,
Before this very house, who seiz'd on you
And would have borne you off. You call'd on gods   295
And men for your assistance. I ran up
And snatch'd you from them, notwithstanding all.
On which account, as I had done you service,
You gave my freedom to me. After that,
You bade me go and fetch your goods and money.   300
You've hasten'd on, fast as you could before.
To frustrate your own deeds.

M. SOSICLES   And did I bid you
Depart a freeman?

MESSENIO   Certainly.   305

M. SOSICLES   And 'tis
Most certain I'm as much a slave myself
As e'er I gave to you your liberty.

Scene 7

(Enter MENAECHMUS EPIDAMNUM, *from Erotium's house)*

M. EPIDAMNUM   Vile woman as you are, tho' you should swear   310
By all that's dear to you that I this day
Bore off that robe and bracelet, yet you never,
No, never should convince me.

MESSENIO   Gods immortal!
What is it that I see?   315

M. SOSICLES   Why, what do you see?

MESSENIO   Why, your resemblance, Sir, as in a mirror.

M. SOSICLES   What is't you mean?

MESSENIO   Your image, and as like
As possible.   320

M. SOSICLES   'Troth, if I know myself,
'Tis not unlike.

M. EPIDAMNUM   Young man, who'er you are,
The gods preserve you! You have sav'd my life.

MESSENIO   Young man, if 'tis not disagreeable,   325
Tell me your name?

M. EPIDAMNUM   You have so much oblig'd me,
You cannot ask what I'd be slow to grant you;
My name's Menaechmus.

M. SOSICLES   Mine's Menaechmus too.   330

M. EPIDAMNUM   I'm a Sicilian, and of Syracuse.

M. SOSICLES   I am the same; it is my native country.

M. EPIDAMNUM   What's that I hear?

M. SOSICLES   You hear the very truth.

MESSENIO   I know this gentleman; he is my master.   335
    I am his servant. But I thought myself
    The other's servant. Sir, (*to* MENAECHMUS SOSICLES) I thought him, you,
    And by so doing gave you some uneasiness.
    If I have said ought foolish or imprudent,
    I pray you pardon me.   340

M. SOSICLES   You're mad, I think.
    Don't you remember that this very day
    You disembark'd with me?

MESSENIO   Nothing more just.
    You are my master. Seek (*to* MENAECHMUS EPIDAMNUM) another servant.   345
    (*To* MENAECHMUS SOSICLES) God save you, Sir! and you, (*to* MENAECHMUS
      EPIDAMNUM) good Sir, adieu!
    This is, I say, Menaechmus.

M. EPIDAMNUM   I say I am.

M. SOSICLES   What comedy is this? You Menaechmus!   350

M. EPIDAMNUM   I am, Sir! And my father's name was Moschus.

M. SOSICLES   And are you then my father's son?

M. EPIDAMNUM   I'm son
    Of my own father, youth. I do not want
    To claim your father, nor to take him from you.   355

MESSENIO   Ye gods! Confirm the unexpected hope
    Which I'm conceiving. These, if I mistake not,
    Are the twin brothers; for they both agree,
    In owning the same father, the same country.
    I'll call aside my master. Sir! Menaechmus!   360

BOTH MEN   Whom is't you want?

MESSENIO   I want but one of you.
    But which of you came with me in the ship?

M. EPIDAMNUM   Not I.

M. SOSICLES   'Twas I.   365

MESSENIO   Why then, 'tis you I want.
    Come this way.

M. SOSICLES   Well, I'm here; what do you want?

MESSENIO   That man is an impostor, Sir, or else
    He's your twin brother. For I never saw   370
    Two men, like one another so exactly.
    Water is, I assure you, not more like
    To water, nor is milk more like to milk,
    Than he is like to you and you to him.
    Besides, he owns himself of the same country   375

And claims, too, the same father. Best accost him
And ask him some few questions.

M. SOSICLES   Your advice
Is right, by Hercules! I thank you for it.
I beg you, give me farther your assistance,   380
And, if you find us brothers you shall have
Your freedom.

MESSENIO   Sir, I hope I shall.

M. SOSICLES   I hope
The same.   385

MESSENIO (*To* MENAECHMUS EPIDAMNUM)   What was't you said? I think it
was
That you are call'd Menaechmus?

M. EPIDAMNUM   Yes.

MESSENIO   But he   390
Is call'd Menaechmus too. In Sicily
You said that you were born, a citizen
Of Syracuse. Why there was he born too.
You've likewise said that Moschus was your father.
Why, Moschus was his father too. And now   395
Is't in the power of both of you to assist me,
And, in assisting me, to assist yourselves.

M. EPIDAMNUM   You have deserv'd so much of me that what
You ask you may command. Free as I am
I'll serve you, just as if I was your slave.   400

MESSENIO   I hope you're just upon the point of finding
That you're twin brothers, born at the same time,
Sons of one father, and one mother too.

M. EPIDAMNUM   You mention wonders. Would you could effect
That which you've given assurance of.   405

MESSENIO   I can.
Come now. To that which I shall ask of you,
Both answer me.

M. EPIDAMNUM   Ask when you please, I'll answer
And not conceal one jot of what I know.   410

MESSENIO   Is then your name Menaechmus?

M. EPIDAMNUM   Yes, I own it.

MESSENIO   And yours the same?

M. SOSICLES   It is.

MESSENIO   You also say   415
Your father's name was Moschus.

M. EPIDAMNUM   Yes, I do.

M. SOSICLES   And mine the same.

MESSENIO   Are you of Syracuse?

M. EPIDAMNUM   Most certainly.   420

MESSENIO   And you?

M. SOSICLES   No doubt of it.

MESSENIO   Hitherto all the marks agree right well.
    But let's go on. What's the most distant thing
    You recollect to have happened in your country? 425

M. EPIDAMNUM   The going with my father to Tarentum
    I'th' way of merchandising; in the crowd
    My straying from my father; after that,
    My being hither brought.

M. SOSICLES   Preserve me, Jupiter! 430

MESSENIO   Why is that exclamation? Hold your peace.
    (*To* MENAECHMUS EPIDAMNUM) Say, when your father from your country
                                   took you,
    What was your age?

M. EPIDAMNUM   Seven years: for I remember 435
    Just at that time my teeth began to shed.
    Nor from that time have I e'er seen my father.

MESSENIO   How many children had your father?

M. EPIDAMNUM   Two,
    If I remember right. 440

MESSENIO   Were you or he
    The elder?

M. EPIDAMNUM   We were both of the same age.

MESSENIO   How can that be?

M. EPIDAMNUM   We both were twins. 445

M. SOSICLES   The gods
    Are pleas'd to bless me—

MESSENIO   If you interrupt me,
    I'll say no more.

M. SOSICLES   Rather than that, I'm silent. 450

MESSENIO   Say, had you both one name?

M. EPIDAMNUM   Not so. My name
    Was, as 'tis now, Menaechmus. But my brother
    They named Sosicles.

M. SOSICLES   I own the proofs. 455
    I cannot hold out longer. I'll embrace him.
    My brother, my twin brother, hail! 'Tis I
    Am Sosicles.

M. EPIDAMNUM   If so, why were you afterwards Menaechmus call'd?

M. SOSICLES   When afterwards we heard 460
    You and your father both were dead, my grandfather,
    Changing my name, gave me the same as yours.

M. EPIDAMNUM   Well, I believe 'tis all just as you say.
    But in your turn now answer me.

M. SOSICLES   Your pleasure. 465

M. EPIDAMNUM   What was our mother's name?

M. SOSICLES   'Twas Theusimarche.

M. EPIDAMNUM All this agree. Hail, my unlook'd-for brother,
Whom after years of absence, I now see.

M. SOSICLES The same all hail to you, my dearest brother, 470
For whom I've search'd till now with so much pains,
And whom I now rejoice to have found at last.

MESSENIO It was on this account the courtezan
Then call'd you by his name and, taking you
For him, she ask'd you to her house to dinner. 475

M. EPIDAMNUM 'Troth, I this day had order'd at her house
A dinner, to my wife unknown, from whom
I filch'd a robe and gave her as a present.

M. SOSICLES Is this the robe you see me with, my brother?

M. EPIDAMNUM How came it in your hands? 480

M. SOSICLES A common woman
Invited me to dine and said 'twas I
That gave it her. I ate a hearty dinner,
Drank freely, entertain'd myself with her,
And got this robe, this bracelet— 485

M. EPIDAMNUM I'm glad, brother,
That you have fared so well on my account;
For when she ask'd you home to dinner with her,
'Twas me she took you for.

MESSENIO What hinders, then, 490
But, as you promis'd me, I should be free?

M. EPIDAMNUM He asks but what is right and just, my brother,
Do it on my account.

M. SOSICLES Be free.

M. EPIDAMNUM I joy, 495
Messenio, that you have obtain'd your freedom.

MESSENIO You see a better hand than yours was wanting
To make me free for life.

M. SOSICLES Since things are thus
As we could wish, let's both return together 500
To our native country.

M. EPIDAMNUM As you please, my brother.
I'll make an auction and sell all I have.
In the meantime, my brother, let's go in.

M. SOSICLES With all my heart. 505

MESSENIO Can you guess what I'd ask?

M. EPIDAMNUM What is it?

MESSENIO That you'd make me auctioneer.

M. EPIDAMNUM 'Tis granted.

MESSENIO Well, Sir, shall I then proclaim 510
The auction straight? And for what day?

M. EPIDAMNUM The seventh.

MESSENIO O yes! O yes! This, Sirs, is to give notice.

The auction of Menaechmus will begin
The seventh of this month, when will be sold   515
Slaves, household goods, farms, houses, and—et cetera.
All may attend that will, and we sell all
For ready money. Sell his wife, besides,
If any purchaser should offer. I scarce think
Our auction will amount to fifty times   520
A thousand sesterces.
(*To the spectators*) Spectators, now
Adieu! and favour us with a loud applause. (*Exeunt*)

Seneca

Lucius Annaeus Seneca (c.4 B.C.–65 A.D.), known as Seneca the Younger, was the only dramatist of importance to appear during the general decline of Roman drama during the last days of the Republic and the early days of the Empire. His plays were written primarily for reading and had little influence on the Roman theater, but to the later humanist writers of the Renaissance they represented the finest examples of classical tragedy. Seneca's repertory of themes of violence and the supernatural provided for Renaissance dramatists a whole catalog of structural conventions and devices to draw on in their attempts to live up to their classical heritage. In addition to his nine tragedies, Seneca wrote a variety of other works, including ten treatises on moral problems, a collection of letters, his NATURAL HISTORY: NATURAL QUESTIONS, and a satire.

Chronology

*c.*4 B.C. Probable year of his birth at Cordova in Spain. He was the son of an aristocratic family; his father was Marcus Annaeus Seneca, the rhetorician.

*c.*1–5 A.D. Brought as a child to Rome, where as a young man he associated intimately with court circles.

*c.*25 Achieved great success as a lawyer and amassed a fortune.

*c.*33 Held the quaestorship under the Emperor Tiberius.

41 Exiled to Corsica through the machinations of Messalina, the third wife of the Emperor Claudius, perhaps because Seneca was the lover of Agrippina, Claudius' current wife.

49 Recalled from Corsica through Agrippina's influence and named tutor to the Young Nero.

54 Nero became emperor. In the early years of his reign Seneca exerted a considerable influence over him; he may even have had a part in Nero's murder of his mother, Agrippina.

62 Offered his fortune to Nero and retired to private life.

65 Convicted on doubtful evidence of taking a part in Piso's conspiracy against Nero and condemned to death. He committed suicide by poisoning.

Selected Bibliography

Arnold, E. V., *Roman Stoicism,* Cambridge, 1911.

Coffey, Michael, "Seneca, Tragedies . . . Report for the Years 1922–1955," *Lustrum: Internationale Forschungsberichte aus dem Bereich des klassischen Altertums,* Göttingen, 1958, 113–186.

Charlton, H. B., *The Senecan Tradition in Renaissance Tragedy*, Manchester, 1946.

Cunliffe, J. W., *The Influence of Seneca on Elizabethan Tragedy*, New York, 1893.

Gummere, R. M., *Seneca the Philosopher and His Modern Message*, Boston, 1922.

Holland, F., *Seneca*, London, 1920.

Lucas, Frank L., *Seneca and Elizabethan Tragedy*, Cambridge, 1922.

Mendell, C. W., *Our Seneca*, New Haven, Conn., 1941

Murray, Gilbert, *The Stoic Philosophy*, New York, 1915.

Pratt, N. T., *Dramatic Suspense in Seneca and His Precursors*, Princeton, N.J., 1937.

Reconstruction of a Roman theater

MEDEA

by Seneca

Translated by Ella Isabel Harris

Characters
MEDEA, *daughter of Aeëtes, king of Colchis, benefactor and divorced wife of Jason*
CHORUS *of Corinthians*
NURSE *of Medea*
CREON, *king of Corinth and father of Creusa*
JASON, *son of Aeson, deposed king of Iolcus, leader of the Argonauts and now in exile from Iolcus*
MESSENGER

Act One

Scene 1

Before the house of MEDEA *and the palace of* CREON *at Corinth*
(*Enter* MEDEA)

MEDEA (*Alone*)   Ye gods of marriage;
Lucina,* guardian of the genial bed;
Pallas, who taught the tamer of the seas
To steer the Argo;* stormy ocean's lord;
Titan,* dividing bright day to the world;   5
And thou three-formed Hecate,* who dost shed
Thy conscious splendor on the hidden rites!
Ye by whom Jason plighted me his troth;
And ye Medea rather should invoke:
Chaos of night eternal; realm opposed   10
To the celestial powers; abandoned souls;
King of the dusky realm; Persephone,*
By better faith betrayed; you I invoke,
But with no happy voice. Approach, approach,
Avenging goddesses with snaky hair.*   15
Holding in blood-stained hands your sulphurous torch!

2 That is, Diana or Luna.
4 The *Argo* was the fabled vessel built by Argus in which Jason and the Argonauts went in search of the golden fleece.
5 The sun.
6 "Three-formed" because she was Luna in heaven, Diana on earth, and Proserpine in Hades.
12 Proserpine, queen of Hades.
15 The Furies.

Come now as horrible as when of yore
Ye stood beside my marriage-bed; bring death
To the new bride, and to the royal seed,
And Creon*; worse for Jason I would ask—   20
Life! Let him roam in fear through unknown lands,
An exile, hated, poor, without a home;
A guest now too well known, let him, in vain,
Seek alien doors, and long for me, his wife!
And, yet a last revenge, let him beget   25
Sons like their father, daughters like their mother!
'Tis done; revenge is even now brought forth—
I have borne sons to Jason. I complain
Vainly, and cry aloud with useless words,
Why do I not attack mine enemies?   30
I will strike down the torches from their hands,
The light from heaven. Does the sun see this,
The author of our race, and still give light?
And, sitting in his chariot, does he still
Run through the accustomed spaces of the sky,   35
Nor turn again to seek his rising place,
And measure back the day? Give me the reins;
Father, let me in thy paternal car
Be borne aloft the winds, and let me curb
With glowing bridle those thy fiery steeds!   40
Burn Corinth; let the parted seas be joined!
This still remains—for me to carry up
The marriage torches to the bridal room,
And, after sacrificial prayers, to slay
The victims on their altars. Seek, my soul—   45
If thou still livest, or if aught endures
Of ancient vigor—seek to find revenge
Through thine own bowels; throw off women's fears,
Intrench thyself in snowy Caucasus.*
All impious deeds Phasis or Pontus* saw,   50
Corinth shall see. Evils unknown and wild,
Hideous, frightful both to earth and heaven,
Disturb my soul,—wounds, and the scattered corpse,
And murder. I remember gentle deeds,
A maid did these; let heavier anguish come,   55
Since sterner crimes befit me now, a wife!
Gird thee with wrath, prepare thine utmost rage,
That fame of thy divorce may spread as far

---

[20] When Jason and Medea were driven out of Thessaly, Jason's homeland, they fled to the court of Creon.
There Creon selected Jason as husband for his daughter Creusa and ordered that Medea be banished.
[49] A mountain range between the Black and Caspian Seas.
[50] Rivers in Colchis, Medea's homeland, where she had used her magic in Jason's behalf to accomplish
a number of deeds against her people and family.

As of thy marriage! Make no long delay.
How dost thou leave thy husband? As thou cam'st. 60
Homes crime built up, by crime must be dissolved.

Scene 2

(*Enter* CHORUS OF CORINTHIANS, *singing the marriage song of* JASON
and CREUSA)

CHORUS Be present at the royal marriage feast,
   Ye gods who sway the scepter of the deep, 65
And ye who hold dominion in the heavens;
With the glad people come, ye smiling gods!
First to the scepter-bearing thunderers*
The white-backed bull shall stoop his lofty head;
The snowy heifer, knowing not the yoke,* 70
Is due to fair Lucina; and to her*
Who stays the bloody hand of Mars, and gives
To warring nations peace, who in her horn
Holds plenty, sacrifice a victim mild.
Thou who at lawful bridals dost preside, 75
Scattering darkness with thy happy torch,
Come hither with slow step and drunk with wine,
Binding thy temples with a rosy crown.
Thou star that bringest in the day and night,
Slow-rising on the lover, ardently 80
For thy clear shining maids and matrons long.
  In comeliness the virgin bride excels bride excels
The Athenian women and the strong-limbed maids
Of Sparta's unwalled town, who on the top
Of high Taÿgetos* try youthful sports; 85
Or those who in the clear Aonian stream,
Or in Alpheus' sacred waters bathe.
The child of the wild thunder, he who tames
And fits the yoke to tigers,* is less fair
Than the Aesonian prince.* The glorious god 90
Who moves the tripod, Dian's brother mild;*
The skilful boxer Pollux; Castor, too,*
Must yield the palm to Jason. O ye gods
Who dwell in heaven, ever may the bride
Surpass all women, he excel all men! 95

[68] Jupiter and Juno.
[70] A white bull which had never known the yoke was traditionally sacrificed to Jupiter.
[71] Venus.
[85] A rugged mountain range in the Peloponnesus.
[89] Dionysus or Bacchus.
[90] Jason, son of Aeson.
[91] Apollo.
[92] The twin sons of Jupiter and Leda.

Before her beauty in the women's choir
The beauty of the other maids grows dim;
So with the sunrise pales the light of stars,
So when the moon with brightness not her own
Fills out her crescent horns, the Pleiads fade.   100
Her cheeks blush like white cloth 'neath Tyrian dyes,*
Or as the shepherd sees the light of stars
Grow rosy with the dawn. O happy one,
Accustomed once to clasp unwillingly
A wife unloved and reckless,* snatched away   105
From that dread Colchian marriage, take thy bride,
The Æolian virgin—'tis her father's will.

  Bright offspring of the thyrsus-bearing god,*
The time has come to light the torch of pine;
With fingers dripping wine flash out the fires,   110
Sound the gay music of the marriage song,
Let the crowd pass their jests; 'tis only she
Who fled her home to wed a stranger guest,
Need steal away into the silent dark.

Act Two

Scene 1

(Enter the NURSE)

MEDEA Alas, the wedding chorus strikes my ears;
Woe, woe to me! I could not hitherto
Believe—can hardly yet believe such wrong.
And this is Jason's deed? Of father, home,   5
And kingdom reft, can he desert me now,
Alone and in a foreign land? Can he
Despise my worth who saw the flames and seas
By my art conquered? thinks, perchance, all crime
Exhausted! Tossed by every wave of doubt,   10
I am distracted, seeking some revenge.
Had he a brother! Ah, he has a bride;
Through her be thrust the steel! Is this enough?
If Grecian or barbarian cities know
Crime that this hand knows not, that crime be done!   15
Thy sins return to mind exhorting thee:*
The stolen treasure of a kingdom, too;

---

101 A famous purple dye of Tyre.
105 Medea.
108 Bacchus.
16 Medea recalls her crimes in Jason's behalf: the theft of the golden fleece; the murder of her brother,
Absyrtus; and the murder of Pelias, Jason's uncle.

Thy little comrade, wicked maid, destroyed,
Torn limb from limb and scattered on the sea
An offering to his father; Pelias old   20
Killed in the boiling cauldron. I have shed
Blood basely, but not yet, not yet have shown
The power of wrath, unhappy love did all.
    Had Jason any choice, by foreign law
And foreign power constrained? He should have bared   25
His breast to feel the sword. O bitter grief,
Speak milder, milder words. Let Jason live;
Mine as he was, if this be possible,
But, if not mine, still let him live secure,
To spare me still the memory of my gift!   30
The fault is Creon's; he abuses power
To annul our marriage, sever strongest ties,
And tear the children from their mother's breast;
Let Creon pay the penalty he owes.
I'll heap his home in ashes, the dark flame   35
Shall reach Malea's dreaded cape,* where ships
Find passage only after long delay.

NURSE   Be silent, I implore thee, hide thy pain
Deep in thy bosom. He who silently
Bears grievous wounds, with patience, and a mind   40
Unshaken, may find vengeance. Hidden wrath
Finds strength, when open hatred loses hope
Of vengeance.

MEDEA   Light is grief that hides itself,
And can take counsel. Great wrongs lie not hid.   45
I am resolved on action.

NURSE   Foster-child,
Restrain thy fury; hardly art thou safe
Though silent.

MEDEA   Fortune tramples on the meek,   50
But fears the brave.

NURSE   When courage is in place
It wins approval.

MEDEA   It can never be
That courage should be out of place.   55

NURSE   To thee,
In thy misfortune, hope points out no way.

MEDEA   The man who cannot hope should naught despair.

NURSE   Colchis is far away, thy husband lost;
Of all thy riches nothing now remains.   60

MEDEA   Medea now remains! Land, sea, sword, fire,
God and the thunderbolt, are found in me.

---

[36] A promontory on the southern extremity of the Peloponnesian peninsula.

NURSE	The king is to be feared.
MEDEA	I claim a king
	For father.
NURSE	Hast thou then no fear of arms?
MEDEA	I, who saw warriors spring from earth?*
NURSE	Thou'lt die!
MEDEA	I wish it.
NURSE	Flee!
MEDEA	Nay, I repent of flight.
NURSE	Thou art a mother.
MEDEA	And thou seest by whom.
NURSE	Wilt thou not fly?
MEDEA	I fly, but first revenge.
NURSE	Vengeance may follow thee.
MEDEA	I may, perchance,
	Find means to hinder it.
NURSE	Restrain thyself
	And cease to threaten madly; it is well
	That thou adjust thyself to fortune's change.
MEDEA	My riches, not my spirit, fortune takes.
	The hinge creaks,—who is this? Creon himself,
	Swelling with Grecian pride. (*The* NURSE *goes out*)

65

70

75

80

Scene 2

(*Enter* CREON *with Attendants.*)

85

CREON   What, is Medea of the hated race
Of Colchian Æëtes,* not yet gone?
Still she is plotting evil; well I know
Her guile, and well I know her cruel hand.
Whom does she spare, or whom let rest secure?
Verily I had thought to cut her off
With the swift sword, but Jason's prayers availed
To spare her life. She may go forth unharmed
If she will set our city free from fear.
Threatening and fierce, she seeks to speak with us;
Attendants, keep her off, bid her be still,
And let her learn at last, a king's commands
Must be obeyed. Go, haste, and take her hence.

90

95

MEDEA   What fault is punished by my banishment?

CREON   A woman innocent doth ask, "What fault?"

100

MEDEA   If thou wilt judge, examine; or if king, Command.

CREON   Unjust or just, a king must be
Obeyed.

MEDEA   An unjust king not long endures.

---

[67] An allusion to the sowing of the dragon teeth by Jason. The teeth immediately sprouted a troup of warriors whom Jason, guided by Medea, set to destroying each other.

[87] Medea's father, king of Colchis.

CREON Go now! To Colchians complain!   ¹⁰⁵
MEDEA   I go;
    Let him who brought me hither take me hence.
CREON Thy words come late, my edict has gone forth.
MEDEA The man who judges, one side still unheard,
    Were hardly a just judge, through he judge justly.   ¹¹⁰
CREON Pelias for listening to thee died, but speak,
    Let me give time to hear so fair a plea.
MEDEA How hard it is to calm a wrathful soul,
    How he who takes the scepter in proud hands
    Deems his own will sufficient, I have learned;   ¹¹⁵
    Have learned it in my father's royal house.
    For though the sport of fortune, suppliant,
    Banished, alone, forsaken, on all sides
    Distressed, my father was a noble king.
    I am descended from the glorious sun.   ¹²⁰
    What lands the Phasis in its winding course
    Bathes, or the Euxine* touches where the sea
    Is freshened by the water from the lakes,
    Or where armed maiden cohorts try their skill
    Beside Thermodon, all these lands are held   ¹²⁵
    Within my father's kingdom, where I dwelt
    Noble and favored, and with princely power.
    He whom kings seek, sought then to wed with me.
    Swift, fickle fortune cast me headlong forth,
    And gave me exile. Put thy thrust in thrones—   ¹³⁰
    Such trust as thou mayst put in what light chance
    Flings here and there at will! Kings have one power,
    A matchless honor time can never take:
    To help the wretched, and to him who asks
    To give a safe retreat. This I have brought   ¹³⁵
    From Colchis, this at least I still can claim:
    I saved the flower of Grecian chivalry,
    Achaian chiefs, the offspring of the gods;
    It is to me they owe their Orpheus
    Whose singing melted rocks and drew the trees;   ¹⁴⁰
    Castor and Pollux are my twofold gift;
    Boreas' sons, and Lynceus whose sharp eye
    Could pierce beyond the Euxine, are my gift,
    And all the Argonauts. Of one alone,
    The chief of chiefs, I do not speak; for him   ¹⁴⁵
    Thou owest me naught; those have I saved for thee,
    This one is mine. Rehearse, now, all my crime;
    Accuse me; I confess; this is my fault—
    I saved the Argo! Had I heard the voice
    Of maiden modesty or filial love,   ¹⁵⁰

¹²² The Black Sea.

Greece and her leaders had regretted it,
And he, thy son-in-law, had fallen first
A victim to the fire-belching bull.*
Let fortune trample on me as she will,
My hand has succored princes, I am glad!   155
Thou hast the recompense for all my crimes.
Condemn me, but give back the cause of crime.
Creon, I own my guilt—guilt known to thee
When first a suppliant I touched thy knees,
And asked with outstretched hands protecting aid.   160
Again I ask a refuge, some poor spot
For misery to hide in; grant a place
Withdrawn, a safe asylum in thy realm,
If I must leave the city.

CREON   I am no prince who rules with cruel sway,   165
Or tramples on the wretched with proud foot.
Have I not shown this true by choosing him
To be my son-in-law who is a man
Exiled, without resource, in fear of foes?
One whom Acastus, king of Thessaly,*   170
Seeks to destroy, that so he may avenge
A father weak with age, bowed down with years ,
Whose limbs were torn asunder? That foul crime
His pious sisters impiously dared,
Tempted by thee;* if thou wilt go away,   175
Jason can then maintain his innocence;
No guiltless blood has stained him, and his hands
Touched not the sword, are yet unstained by thee.
Foul instigator of all evil deeds,
With woman's wantonness in daring aught,   180
And man's courageous heart—and void of shame,
Go, purge our kingdom; take thy deadly herbs,
Free us from fear; dwelling in other lands
Afar, invoke the gods.

MEDEA   Thou bidst me go?   185
Give back the ship and comrade of my flight.
Why bid me go alone? Not so I came.
If thou fear war, both should go forth, nor choice
Be made between two equally at fault:
That old man* fell for Jason's sake, impute   190
To Jason flight, rapine, a brother slain,

---

153 The first task set to Jason by Aeëtes of Colchis was the yoking of the fire-breathing bulls. With the
   help of a charm provided by Medea he accomplished the task without injury.
170 The son of Pelias, he has demanded that Creon surrender Jason and Medea to him.
175 Medea's strategy for murdering Pelias involved persuading Pelias' daughters, who wished Medea to
   restore Pelias to youth as she had already restored Jason's father, that they must first kill Pelias. But
   when the daughters had stabbed him, Medea did not restore him.
190 Pelias.

And a deserted father; not all mine
The crimes to which a husband tempted me;
'Tis true I sinned, but never for myself.

CREON   Thou shouldst be gone, why waste the time with words?   195

MEDEA   I go, but going make one last request:
Let not a mother's guilt drag down her sons.

CREON   Go, as a father I will succor them,
And with a father's care.

MEDEA   By future hopes,   200
By the king's happy marriage, by the strength
Of thrones, which fickle fortune sometimes shakes,
I pray thee grant the exile some delay
That she, perchance about to die, may press
A last kiss on her children's lips.   205

CREON   Thou seekst
Time to commit new crime.

MEDEA   In so brief time
What crime were possible?

CREON   No time too short   210
For him who would do ill.

MEDEA   Dost thou deny
To misery short space for tears?

CREON   Deep dread
Warns me against thy prayer; yet I will grant   215
One day in which thou mayst prepare for flight.

MEDEA   Too great the favor! Of the time allowed,
Something withdraw. I would depart in haste.

CREON   Before the coming day is ushered in
By Phœbus, leave the city or thou diest.   220
The bridal calls me, and I go to pay
My vows to Hymen.* (*Exeunt*)

Scene 3

CHORUS   He rashly ventured who was first to make
In his frail boat a pathway through the deep;
Who saw his native land behind him fade   225
In distance blue; who to the raging winds
Trusted his life, his slender keel between
The paths of life and death. Our fathers dwelt
In an unspotted age, and on the shore
Where each was born he lived in quietness,   230
Grew old upon his father's farm content;
With little rich, he knew no other wealth
Than his own land afforded. None knew yet
The changing constellations, nor could use

---

222 God of marriage.

As guides the stars that paint the ether; none   235
Had learned to shun the rainy Hyades;*
None had as yet to Goat, or Northern Wain
That follows slow by old Boötes driven,
Or Boreas, or Zephyr, given names.
Rash Tiphys* was the first to tempt the deep   240
With spreading canvas; for the winds to write
New laws; to furl the sail; or spread it wide
When sailors longed to fly before the gale,
And the red topsail fluttered in the breeze.
The world so wisely severed by the seas   245
The pine of Thessaly united, bade
The ocean suffer scourgings at our hands,
And distant waters bring us unknown fears.
The ill-starred ship paid heavy penalty
When the two cliffs, the gateway of the sea,   250
Moved as though smitten by the thunderbolt,
And the imprisoned waters smote the stars.*
Bold Tiphys paled, and from his trembling hand
Let fall the rudder; Orpheus' music died,
His lyre untouched; the Argo lost her voice.   255
When, belted by her girdle of wild dogs,
The maid of the Sicilian straits* gave voice
From all her mouths, who feared not at her bark?
Who did not tremble at the witching song
With which the Sidens charmed the Ausonian sea?   260
The Thracian Orpheus' lyre had almost forced
Those hinderers of ships to follow him!
What was the journey's prize? The golden fleece,
Medea, fiercer than the raging flood,—
Worthy reward for those first mariners!   265
    The sea forgets its former wrath; submits
To the new laws; and not alone the ship
Minerva builded, manned by sons of kings,
Finds rowers; other ships may sail the deep.
Old metes are moved, new city walls spring up   270
On distant soil, and nothing now remains
As it has been in the much-traveled world.

---

236 A cluster of five stars associated by the ancients with rain. The following are also constellations, while
the Boreas and Zephyr are winds.

240 The pilot of the *Argo*.

252 The entrance to the Black Sea was blocked by two floating islands called the Symplegades, or Clashing
Islands, because they clashed together to crush objects passing between them. By luring the islands to
close upon a dove, the Argonauts slipped through while the islands were drawing back, but not without
having the stern of the *Argo* grazed.

257 An allusion to the feat by which Orpheus saved the Argonauts by playing more sweetly than the
sirens sang; the sirens customarily lured sailors to their death with their songs.

The cold Araxes' stream the Indian drinks;
The Persian quaffs the Rhine; a time shall come
With the slow years, when ocean shall strike off   275
The chains from earth, and a great world shall then
Lie opened; Tiphys shall win other lands—
Another Tiphys—Thule cease to be
Earth's utmost bound.

Act Three

Scene 1

(*Enter* MEDEA *and The* NURSE)

NURSE   Stay, foster-child, why fly so swiftly hence?
Restrain thy wrath! curb thy impetuous haste!
As a Bacchante, frantic with the god
And filled with rage divine, uncertain walks   5
The top of snowy Pindus or the peak
Of Nysa, so Medea wildly goes
Hither and thither; on her face the mark
Of frenzied rage, her visage flushed, her breast
Shaken by sobs. She cries aloud, her eyes   10
Are drowned in scalding tears; again she laughs;
All passions surge within her angry heart.
Where will she fling the burden of her soul?
She hesitates, she threatens, storms, complains,
Where falls her vengeance? where will break this wave   15
Of fury? Passion overflows! she plans
No easy crime, no ordinary deed.
Herself she will surpass; I mark old signs
Of raging; something terrible she plans,
Some deed inhuman, devilish, and wild.   20
Ye gods, avert the horrors I foresee!
MEDEA   Wretch, dost thou seek how far to show thy hate?
Imitate love! And must I then endure
Without revenge the royal marriage-torch?
Shall this day prove unfruitful, sought and gained   25
Only by earnest effort? While the earth
Hangs free within the heavens; while the vault
Of heaven sweeps round the earth with changeless change;
While the sands lie unnumbered; while the day
Follows the sun, the night brings up the stars;   30
Arcturus* never wet in ocean's wave
Rolls round the pole; which rivers seaward flow,
My hate shall never cease to seek revenge.

³¹ The brightest star in the constellation Boötes.

Did ever fierceness of a ravening beast;
Or Scylla or Charybdis* sucking down   35
The waters of the wild Ausonian*
And the Sicilian sea; or Ætna fierce,
That holds imprisoned great Enceladus*
Breathing forth flame, so glow as I with threats?
Not the swift rivers, nor the storm-tossed sea,   40
Nor wind-blown ocean, nor the force of flame
By storm-wind fanned, can imitate my wrath.
I will o'erthrow and bring to naught the world!
Did Jason fear the king? Thessalian war?
True love fears naught. Or was he forced to yield,   45
And gave consent unwillingly? But still
He might have sought his wife for one farewell.
This too he feared to do. He might have gained
From Creon some delay of banishment.
One day is granted for my two sons' sake!   50
I do not make complaint of too short time,
It is enough for much; this day shall see
What none shall ever hide. I will attack
The very gods, and shake the universe!

NURSE   Lady, thy spirit so disturbed by ills   55
Restrain, and let thy storm-tossed soul find rest.

MEDEA   Rest I can never find until I see
All dragged with me to ruin; all shall fall
When I do;—so to share one's woe is joy.

NURSE   Think what thou hast to fear if thou persist; 60
No one can safely fight with princely power. (*The* NURSE *withdraws*)

Scene 2

(*Enter* JASON)

JASON   The lot is ever hard; bitter is fate,
Equally bitter if it slay or spare;
God gives us remedies worse than our ills.   65
Would I keep faith with her I deem my wife
I must expect to die; would I shun death
I must forswear myself. Not fear of death
Has conquered honor, but love full of fear
Knowing the father's death involves the sons.   70
O holy Justice, if thou dwell in heaven,
I call on thee to witness that the sons
Vanquish their father! Say the mother's love

---

35 The former was a rock, the latter a whirlpool; and they guard the strait between Sicily and Italy. They
  were also personified as female monsters.
36 The Tyrrenian Sea.
38 One of the titans who attempted to dethrone Jupiter; he was buried under Sicily.

Is fierce and spurns the yoke, she still will deem
Her children of more worth than marriage joys.   75
I fain would go to her with prayers, and lo,
She starts at sight of me, her look grows wild,
Hatred she shows and grief.

MEDEA   Jason, I flee!
I flee, it is not new to change my home,   80
The cause of banishment alone is new;
I have been exiled hitherto for thee.
I go, as thou compellst me, from thy home,
But whither shall I go? Shall I, perhaps,
Seek Phasis, Colchis, and my father's realm   85
Whose soil is watered by a brother's blood?*
What land dost thou command me seek? what sea
The Euxine's jaws through which I led that band
Of noble princes when I followed thee,
Adulterer, through the Symplegades?   90
Little Iolchos? Tempe? Thessaly?
Whatever way I opened up for thee
I closed against myself. Where shall I go?
Thou drivest into exile, but hast given
No place of banishment. I will go hence.   95
The king, Creusa's father, bids me go,
And I will do his bidding. Heap on me
Most dreadful punishment, it is my due.
With cruel penalties let the king's wrath
Pursue thy mistress, load my hands with chains,   100
And in a dungeon of eternal night
Imprison me—'tis less than I deserve!
Ungrateful one, recall the fiery bull;
The earth-born soldiers, who at my command
Slew one another; and the longed-for spoils   105
Of Phrixus' ram,* whose watchful guardian,
The sleepless dragon, at my bidding slept;
The brother slain; the many, many crimes
In one crime gathered. Think how, led by me,
By me deceived, that old man's daughters dared   110
To slay their aged father, dead for aye!
By thy hearth's safety, by thy children's weal,
By the slain dragon, by these blood-stained hands
I never spared from doing aught for thee,
By thy past fears, and by the sea and sky   115
Witnesses of our marriage, pity me!

---

[86] Having killed her brother, Absyrtus, Medea had scattered his remains to retard Aeëtes' pursuit of Jason
and herself.

[106] Having escaped from Boeotia on a golden-fleeced ram, Phrixus reached Colchis and there sacrificed the
ram to Jupiter and gave his fleece to Aeëtes, who hung it in a tree sacred to Mars.

Happy thyself, make me some recompense!
Of all the ravished gold the Scythians brought
From far, as far as India's burning plains,
Wealth our wide palace hardly could contain, 120
So that we hung our groves with gold, I took
Nothing. My brother only bore I thence,
And him for thee I sacrificed. I left
My country, father, brother, maiden shame:
This was my marriage portion; give her own 125
To her who goes an exile.

JASON When angry Creon thought to have thee slain,
Urged by my prayers, he gave thee banishment.

MEDEA I looked for a reward; the gift I see
Is exile. 130

JASON While thou mayst fly, fly in haste!
The wrath of kings is ever hard to bear.

MEDEA Thou giv'st me such advice because thou lov'st
Creusa, wouldst divorce a hated wife!

JASON And does Medea taunt me with my loves? 135

MEDEA More—treacheries and murders.

JASON   Canst thou charge
Such sins to me?

MEDEA   All I have ever done.

JASON It only needs that I should share the guilt 140
Of these thy crimes!

MEDEA   Thine are they, thine alone;
He is the criminal who reaps the fruit.
Though all should brand thy wife with infamy,
Thou shouldst defend and call her innocent: 145
She who has sinned for thee, toward thee hold pure.

JASON To me my life is an unwelcome gift
Of which I am ashamed.

MEDEA   Who is ashamed
To owe his life to me can lay it down. 150

JASON For thy sons' sake control thy fiery heart.

MEDEA I will have none of them, I cast them off,
Abjure them; shall Creusa to my sons
Give brothers?

JASON   To an exile's wretched sons 155
A mighty queen will give them.

MEDEA   Never come
That evil day that mingles a great race
With race unworthy,—Phœbus' glorious sons
With sons of Sisyphus.* 160

JASON   What, cruel one,
Wouldst thou drag both to banishment? Away!

---

160 Aeëtes traced to Apollo-Phoebus; Creon was a descendant of Sisyphus.

MEDEA	Creon has heard my prayer.
JASON	What can I do?
MEDEA	For me? Some crime perhaps.

JASON   Two wrathful kings*
    I fear.

MEDEA   Medea's wrath is still more fierce!
    Let us essay our power, the victor's prize
    Be Jason.

JASON   Passion-weary, I submit;
    Thou too shouldst fear a lot so often tried.

MEDEA   Fortune has ever served me faithfully.

JASON   Acastus comes.

MEDEA   Creon's a nearer foe,
    Flee thou from both. Medea does not ask
    That thou shouldst arm thyself against the king,
    Or soil thy hands with murder of thy kin;
    Flee with me innocent.

JASON   Who will oppose
    If double war ensue, and the two kings
    Join forces?

MEDEA '   Add to them the Colchian troops
    And King Æëtes, Scythian hosts and Greeks,
    Medea conquers all!

JASON   I greatly fear
    A scepter's power.

MEDEA   Do not covet it.

JASON   We must cut short our converse, lest it breed
    Suspicion.

MEDEA   Now from high Olympus send
    Thy thunder, Jupiter; stretch forth thy hand,
    Prepare thy lightning, from the riven clouds
    Make the world tremble, nor with careful hand
    Spare him or me; whichever of us dies
    Dies guilty; thy avenging thunderbolt
    Cannot mistake the victim.

JASON   Try to speak
    More sanely; calm thyself. If aught can aid
    Thy flight from Creon's house, thou needst but ask.

MEDEA   My soul is strong enough, and wont to scorn
    The wealth of kings; this boon alone I crave,
    To take my children with me when I go;
    Into their bosoms I would shed my tears,
    New sons are thine.

JASON   Would I might grant thy prayer;
    Paternal love forbids me, Creon's self
    Could not compel me to it. They alone

[166] That is, Creon and Acastus, the son of Pelias.

Lighten the sorrow of a grief-parched soul.
For them I live, I sooner would resign 210
Breath, members, light.
MEDEA (*Aside*)   'Tis well! He loves his sons,
This, then, the place where he may feel a wound!
(*To* JASON) Before I go, thou wilt, at least, permit
That I should give my sons a last farewell, 215
A last embrace? But one thing more I ask:
If in my grief I've poured forth threatening words,
Retain them not in mind; let memory hold
Only my softer speech, my words of wrath
Obliterate. 220
JASON   I have erased them all
From my remembrance. I would counsel thee
Be calm, act gently; calmness quiets pain. (*Exit* JASON)

Scene 3

(*Enter the* NURSE)

MEDEA   He's gone! And can it be he leaves me so, 225
Forgetting me and all my guilt? Forgot?
Nay, never shall Medea be forgot!
Up! Act! Call all thy power to aid thee now;
This fruit of crime is thine, to shun no crime!
Deceit is useless, so they fear my guile. 230
Strike where they do not dream thou canst be feared.
Medea, haste, be bold to undertake
The possible—yea, that which is not so!
Thou, faithful nurse, companion of my griefs
And varying fortunes, aid my wretched plans. 235
I have a robe, gift of the heavenly powers,
An ornament of a king's palace, given
By Phœbus to my father as a pledge
Of sonship; and a necklace of wrought gold;
And a bright diadem, inlaid with gems, 240
With which they used to bind my hair. These gifts,
Endued with poison by my magic arts,
My sons shall carry for me to the bride.
Pay vows to Hecate, bring the sacrifice,
Set up the altars. Let the mounting flame 245
Envelop all the house. (*Exeunt*)

Scene 4

CHORUS   Fear not the power of flame, nor swelling gale,
Nor hurtling dart, nor cloudy wind that brings
The winter storms; fear not when Danube sweeps

Unchecked between his widely severed shores,   250
Nor when the Rhone hastes seaward, and the sun
Has broken up the snow upon the hills,
        And Hæmus* flows in rivers.
A wife deserted, loving while she hates,
Fear greatly; blindly burns her anger's flame,   255
She cares not to be ruled, nor bears the curb,
Nor fears to die; she courts the hostile swords.
Ye gods, we ask your grace divine for him
Who safely crossed the seas; the ocean's lord
Is angry for his conquered kingdom's sake;   260
        Spare Jason, we entreat!
Th' impetuous youth who dared to drive the car
Of Phœbus, keeping not the wonted course,
Died in the heavenly fires himself had lit.*
Few are the evils of the well-known way;   265
Seek the old paths your fathers safely trod,
The sacred federations of the world
        Keep still inviolate.
The men who dipped the oars of that brave ship;
Who plundered of their shade the sacred groves   270
Of Pelion; passed between the unstable cliffs;
Endured so many hardships on the deep;
And cast their anchor on a savage coast,
Passing again with ravished foreign gold,
Atoned with fearful death for dire wrong   275
        To Ocean's sacred laws.
The angry deep demanded punishment:
To an unskilful pilot Tiphys gave
The rudder. On a foreign coast he fell,
Far from his father's kingdom, and he lies   280
With nameless shades, under a lowly tomb.
Becalmed in her still harbor Aulis held
Th' impatient ships, remembering in wrath
        The king that she lost thence. *
Sweet voiced Camena's son,* who touched his lyre   285
So sweetly that the floods stood still, the winds
Were silent, and the birds forgot to sing,
And forests followed him, on Thracian fields
Lies dead, his head borne down by Hebrus' stream.
He touched again the Styx and Tartarus,   290
        But not again returns.

253 A lofty mountain range to the north of Greece.
264 Phaëton.
284 Tiphys, the unfortunate pilot of the *Argo*, was king of Aulis. After his death Aulis was hostile to all
    ships; for example, the bay of Aulis becalmed the Greek fleet on its way to Troy.
285 Orpheus.

Alcides* overthrew the north wind's sons;
He slew that son of Neptune who could take
Unnumbered forms; but after he had made
Peace over land and sea, and opened wide   295
The realm of Dis, lying on Œta's top
He gave his body to the cruel fire,
Destroyed by his wife's gift—the fatal robe
          Poisoned with Centaur's blood.
Ancæus* fell a victim to the boar   300
Of Caledonia; Meleager slew
His mother's brother, perished by the hand
Of his own mother. They have merited
Their lot, but what the crime that he atoned
Whom great Alcides sought so long in vain,   305
The tender Hylas drawn beneath safe waves?*
Go now, brave soldiers, boldly plow the main,
          But fear the gentle streams.
Idmon* the serpents buried in the sands
Of Libya, though he knew the future well.   310
Mopsus, to others true, false to himself,
Fell far from Thebes; and if the seer spoke true,
Peleus must wander exiled from his realm;
And Nauplius, seeking injury to the Greeks
By his deceitful beacon fires, shall fall   315
Into the ocean; Palamedes, too,
Shall suffer, dying for his father's sin.
Oïleus, smitten by the thunderbolt,
Shall perish on the sea; Admetus' wife*
To save her husband's life shall give her own.   320
He who commanded that the golden spoil
Be carried in the ships had traveled far,
But, plunged in seething cauldron, Pelias died*
In narrow limits. 'Tis enough, ye gods;
          Ye have avenged the sea!   325

292 Another name for Hercules.

300 Both Ancaeus and Meleager were Argonauts.

306 Hylas was seized by water nymphs who were fascinated by his beauty. Hercules, who loved him, went
in search of him and was left behind by the Argonauts.

309 Another Argonaut, Idmon was the son of Apollo and Asteria and, despite his prophetic gifts, was
killed by a serpent (according to Seneca) and not, as tradition has it, by a boar. The following heroes,
too, were Argonauts. Mopsus was another soothsayer and was killed by the bite of a snake. Peleus, the
father of Achilles, died in exile. Nauplius, to avenge the death of his son Palamedes, who was put to
death by the Greeks on false charges, tried to lure the Greek fleet to destruction with misleading beacon
fires. When Ulysses, his arch-enemy, escaped, he threw himself into the ocean. Oïleus, the father of
Ajax, was destroyed at sea by Pallas and Neptune for his defiance of the gods.

319 Alcestis.

323 When Pelias' daughters had stabbed him, Medea had him placed in a boiling cauldron, ostensibly to
restore him. The cauldron finished the job.

Act Four

Scene 1

(Enter the NURSE*)*

NURSE I shrink with horror! Ruin threatens us!
How terribly her wrath inflames itself!
Her former force awakes, thus I have seen
Medea raging and attacking God,   5
Compelling heaven. Greater crime than then
She now prepares. No sooner had she sought
Wildly her fatal shrine than she put forth
Her every power, and what before she feared
She does; lets loose all ills, mysterious arts.   10
With her left hand the dismal sacrifice
Preparing, she invokes whatever ills
The Libyan sands with their fierce heat create,
Or frost-bound Taurus* with perpetual snow
Encompasses. Drawn by her magic spell,   15
Come from their desert holes a scaly host.
The serpent drags his heavy length along,
Darts his forked tongue, and seeks his destined prey.
Hearing her incantation, he draws back
And knots his swelling body coiling it.—   20
"They are but feeble poisons earth brings forth,
And harmless darts," she says. "heaven's ills I seek.
Now is the time for deeper sorcery.
The dragon like a torrent shall descend,*
Whose mighty folds the Great and Lesser Bear   25
Know well (the Great Bear o'er the Phrygians shines,
The Less o'er Tyre); Ophiuchus shall loose
His grasp, and poison flow. Come at my call,
Python, who dared to fight twin deities.
The Hydra once cut off by Hercules,   30
Accustomed from its wounds to gain fresh strength,
Shall come. Thou ever watchful Colchian one,
Be present with rest—thou, who first slept
Lulled by my incantations." When the brood
Of serpents has been called she blends the juice   35
Of poisonous herbs; all Eryx' pathless heights*
Bear, or the snow-capped top of Caucasus
Wet with Prometheus' blood, where winter reigns;*

14 A mountain range in southern Asia Minor.

24 There follows an invocation of monsters, the first three of which are, additionally, constellations. Python was the huge serpent that sprang from the slime left when the flood subsided and that Apollo killed. Hydra was a monster of Lerna with nine heads and was killed by Hercules as his second labor. The "Colchian one" was the dragon that guarded the fleece.

36 A mountain in Sicily.

38 Prometheus was chained to a rock in the Caucasus.

All that the rich Arabians use to tip
Their poisoned shafts, or the light Parthians,   40
Or warlike Medes; all Suebian witches cull
In the Hyrcanian forests in the north;
All poisons that the earth brings forth in spring
When birds are nesting; or when winter cold
Has torn away the beauty of the groves   45
And bound the world in icy manacles.
Whatever herb gives flower the cause of death,
Or juice of twisted root, her hands have culled.
These on Thessalian Athos grew, and those
On mighty Pindus; on Pangæus' height   50
She cut the tender leaves with bloody scythe.
These Tigris nurtured with its eddies deep,
The Danube those; Hydaspes rich in gems
Flowing with current warm through levels dry,
Bætis that gives its name to neighboring lands   55
And meets the western ocean languidly,
Have nurtured these. The knife cut those at dawn;
These other herbs at dead of night were reaped;
And these were plucked with the enchanted nail.
Death-dealing plants she chooses, wrings the blood   60
Of serpents, and she takes ill-omened birds,
The sad owl's heart, the quivering entrails cut
From the horned owl living—sorts all these.
In some the eager force of flame is found,
In some the bitter cold of sluggish ice;   65
To these she adds the venom of her words
As greatly to be feared. But lo, I hear
The sound of her mad footstep and her song.
Earth trembles when she hears.

Scene 2

Before the altar of Hecate   70
(*Enter* MEDEA)

MEDEA   Lo, I invoke you, all ye silent shades,
Infernal Gods, blind Chaos, sunless home
Of shadowy Dis, and squalid caves of Death
Bound by the banks of Tartarus. Lost souls,   75
For this new bridal leave your wonted toil.
Stand still, thou whirling wheel, Ixion* touch
Again firm ground; come, Tantalus,* and drink
Unchecked the wave of the Pirenian fount.
Let heavier punishment on Creon wait: 80

[77] For his insult to Juno, Ixion was whirled on a wheel in Hades.
[78] Because of his sin against the gods, Tantalus was doomed to suffer endless hunger and thirst in Hades.

Thou stone of Sisyphus,* worn smooth, roll back;
And ye Danaïdes* who strive in vain
To fill your leaking jars, I need your aid.
Come at my invocation, star of night,*
Endued with form most horrible, nor threat   85
With single face, thou three-formed deity!
  For thee, according to my country's use,
With hair unfilleted and naked feet
I've trod the lonely groves; called forth the rain
From cloudless skies; have driven back the sea;   90
And forced the ocean to withdraw its waves.
Earth sees heaven's laws confused, the sun and stars
Shining together, and the two Bears wet
In the forbidden ocean. I have changed
The circle of the seasons:—at my word   95
Earth flourishes with summer; Ceres* sees
A winter harvest; Phasis' rushing stream
Flows to its source; and Danube that divides
Into so many mouths restrains its flood
Of waters—hardly moving past its shores.   100
The winds are silent; but the waters speak,
The wild seas roar; the home of ancient groves
Loses its leafy shade; and day returns
At my command; the sun stands still in heaven.
My incantations move the Hyades.*   105
It is thy hour, Dian.
  For thee my bloody hands have wrought this crown
Nine times by serpents girt; those knotted snakes
Rebellious Typhon* bore, who made revolt
Against Jove's kingdom; Nessus gave this blood   110
When dying;* Œta's funeral pyre provides
These ashes which have drunk the poisoned blood
Of dying Hercules; and here thou seest
Althea's vengeful brand,* she sacrificed
A mother's to a sister's love. These quills   115
The Harpies left within some trackless cave,

---

[81] For his disobedience to the gods, Sisyphus was given the endless toil of rolling a huge stone up a hill, only to have it roll down again.

[82] Their punishment for killing their husbands was filling a bottomless cistern in Hades with water carried in cracked jars.

[84] Diana.

[96] Goddess of agriculture.

[105] A storm-bringing constellation.

[109] One of the rebellious giants.

[111] When dying, Nessus gave his blood to Deianira to charm Hercules into remaining at home; but the shirt she anointed with the blood poisoned Hercules.

[114] Althea killed her son by lighting the brand which protected his life.

Their refuge when they fled from Zetes' wrath;*
And these were dropped by the Stymphalian birds*
That felt the wound of arrows dipped in blood
Of the Lernæan Hydra.   120
    The altars find a voice, the tripod moves,
Stirred by the favoring goddess. Her swift car
I see approach—not the full-orbed that rolls
All night through heaven; but as, with darkened light,
Her orb contracted, with wan face she moves   125
Through night's dark skies, vexed by Thessalian charms.
So, pale one, from thy torch shed murky light,
Affright the nations that they clash for thee
Corinthian cymbals.* Here I pay to thee,
On altars made of turf and red with blood,   130
These solemn rites; have stolen from the tomb
This torch that gives its baleful funeral light;
To thee with bowed head I have made my prayer;
And in accordance with funeral use,
Have filleted my loosened hair, have plucked   135
This branch that grows beside the Stygian wave;
Like a wild Mænad, laying bare my breast,
With sacred knife I cut for thee my arm;
My blood is on the altars! Hand, learn well
To use the knife and shed blood dear to thee.   140
See, from the wound, the sacred stream flows forth,
Daughter of Perses,* have I asked too oft
Thine aid? Recall no more my former prayers.
Today as always I invoke thine aid
For Jason only! Ah, endue this robe   145
With such a baleful power that the bride
May feel at its first touch consuming fire
Of serpent's poison in her inmost veins;
For fire flames hid in the bright gold, a gift
Prometheus gave and taught me how to store—   150
He now atones his daring theft from heaven
With tortured vitals.* Mulciber has given
This flame,* and I in sulphur nurtured it;
I brought a spark from the destroying fire
Of Phaëton; I have the flame breathed forth   155
By the Chimæra,* and the fire I snatched

---

[117] To protect Phineus, Zetes and Calaïs had driven away the Harpies, monsters who were half-bird, half-woman.

[118] Monstrous creatures that haunted a pool near Stymphalus in Arcadia.

[129] Particularly sonorous cymbals.

[142] Still Diana.

[152] Prometheus stole fire from heaven and gave it to man.

[153] Mulciber (Vulcan) gave sulphurous fires to Medea for her magic.

[156] A monster combining a lion, dragon, and goat; it breathed fire.

From Colchis' savage bull; and mixed with these
Medusa's venom.* I have bade all keep
Their poison unrevealed; now, Hecate, add
The sting to poison, keep the seeds of flame 160
Hid in my gift; let them deceive the sight
Nor burn the touch; but let them penetrate
Her very heart and veins, melt all her limbs,
Consume her bones in smoke. Her burning hair
Shall glow more brightly than the nuptial torch! 165
My vows are heard, and Hecate thrice has barked,
And shaken fire from her gleaming brand.
   'Tis finished! Call my sons. My royal gifts,
Ye shall be borne by them to the new bride.
Go, go, my sons, a hapless mother's brood, 170
Placate with gifts and prayers your father's wife!
But come again with speed, that I may know
A last embrace! (*She exits*)

Scene 3

CHORUS   Where hastes the blood-stained Mænad, headlong driven
By angry love? What mischief plots her rage? 175
With wrath her face grows rigid; her proud head
She fiercely shakes, and dares defiantly
Threaten the king.
Who would believe her exiled from the realm?
Her cheeks glow crimson, pallor puts to flight 180
The red, no color lingers on her face;
Her steps are driven to and fro as when
A tigress rages, of her young bereft,
Beside the Ganges in the gloomy woods.
Medea knows not how to curb her love 185
Or hate. Now love and hate together rage.
When will she leave the fair Pelasgian fields,
The wicked Colchian one, and free from fear
Our king and kingdom? Drive with no slow rein
Thy car, Diana; let the sweet night hide 190
The sunlight. Hesperus,* end the dreaded day.

---

[158] Medusa, one of the Gorgons, had the power to petrify whatever looked at her. She was slain by Perseus, and Medea used her gall in her magic.
[191] Evening star.

Act Five

Scene 1

(Enter a MESSENGER*)*

MESSENGER *(in haste)*   All are destroyed, the royal empire falls,
  Father and child lie in one funeral pyre.
CHORUS   Destroyed by what deceit?
MESSENGER   That which is wont   5
  To ruin princes—gifts.
CHORUS   Could these work harm?
MESSENGER   I myself wonder, and can hardly deem
  The wrong accomplished, though I know it done.
CHORUS   How did it happen?   10
MESSENGER   A destructive fire
  Spreads everywhere as at command; even now
  The city is in fear, the palace burned.
CHORUS   Let water quench the flames.
MESSENGER   It will not these,   15
  As by a miracle floods feed the fire.
  The more we fight it so much more it glows.

Scene 2

(Enter MEDEA, *the* NURSE, *and* MEDEA'S *two Sons)*

NURSE   Up! up! Medea! Swiftly flee the land
  Of Pelops;* seek in haste a distant shore.   20
MEDEA   Shall I fly? I? Were I already gone
  I would return for this, that I might see
  These new betrothals. Dost thou pause, my soul,
  And shrink to follow up thy first success?
  This joy's but the beginning of revenge.   25
  Thou still dost love if thou art satisfied
  To widow Jason. For this work prepare:
  Honor begone and maiden modesty,—
  It were a light revenge pure hands could yield.
  Strengthen thy drooping spirit, stir up wrath,   30
  Drain from thy heart its all of ancient force,
  Thy deeds till now call love; awake, and act,
  That they may see how light, how little worth,
  All former crime—the prelude of revenge!
  What was there great my novice hands could dare?   35
  What was the madness of my girlhood days?
  I am Medea now, through crime made strong.
  Rejoice, because through thee thy brother died;
  Rejoice, because through thee his limbs were torn;
  Through thee thy father lost the golden fleece;   40

<hr>

[20] Peloponnesus, in which Corinth was located.

That, armed by thee, his daughters Pelias slew.
Find thou a way, revenge. No novice hand
Thou bring'st to crime; what wilt thou do; what dart
Let fly against thy treacherous enemy?
I know not what of crime my madness plots, 45
Nor yet dare I confess it to myself!
In folly I made haste—would that my foe
Had children by this other! Mine are his,
We'll say Creusa bore them! 'Tis enough;
Through them my heart at last finds just revenge; 50
My soul must be prepared for this last crime.
Ye who were once my children, mine no more,
Pay ye the forfeit for your father's crimes.
Awe strikes my spirit and benumbs my hand;
My heart beats wildly; vanished is my rage, 55
And mother love, returning, now drives out
The hatred of the wife. I shed their blood?
My children's blood? Give better counsel, rage!
Be far from thee this crime! What guilt is theirs?
Is Jason not their father?—guilt enough! 60
And, greater guilt, Medea calls them sons.
They are not sons of mine, so let them die!
Nay, rather let them perish since they are!
But they are innocent!—my brother was!
Waverest thou? Do tears make wet thy cheek? 65
Do wrath and love like adverse tides impel
Now here, now there? As when the winds wage war
And the wild waves against each other smite,
And warring tides run high, and ocean raves,
My heart is beaten, and love drives out wrath, 70
As wrath drives love. My anger dies in love.
Dear sons, sole solace of a storm-tossed house,
Come hither, lock your arms about my neck;
You may be safe for him, if safe for me!
But I am driven into exile, flight; 75
Torn from my bosom weeping, soon they'll go
Lamenting for my kisses—let them die
For father and for mother! Once again
Rage swells, hate burns; again the fury seeks
Th' unwilling hand—I follow where wrath leads. 80
Would that the children that made proud the heart
Of Niobe were mine, that I had borne
Twice seven sons! In bearing only two
I have been cursed! And yet it is enough
For father, brother, that I have borne two.— 85
Where does that horde of furies haste? whom seek?
From whom prepare their fires? or for whom

Brandish the infernal band the bloody torch?
The huge snake hisses writhing; as they lash
Their serpent scourges; with her hostile brand   90
Whom does Megæra* seek? What dim-seen shade
Is that which hither brings its scattered limbs?
It is my brother, and he seeks revenge;
I grant it, thrust the torches in my eyes;
Kill, burn; the furies have me in their power!   95
Brother, command the avenging goddesses
To leave me, and the shades to seek their place
In the infernal regions without fear;
Here leave me to myself, and use this hand
That held the sword—your soul has found revenge. (*Kills one of her sons*)   100
What means this sudden noise? They come in arms
And seek to slay me. Having thus begun
My murders, I will go upon the roof,
Come, follow thou, I'll take the dead with me.
Strike now, my soul, nor longer hide thy power,   105
But show the world thy strength.
              (*She goes out with the nurse and the living boy, and carries
                   with her the body of her dead son*)

Scene 3

(JASON *enters in the foreground;* MEDEA *with the children appears upon the roof*)
JASON   Ye faithful ones, who share   110
   In the misfortunes of your harassed king,
   Hasten to take the author of these deeds.
   Come hither, hither, cohorts of brave men;
   Bring up your weapons; overthrow the house.
MEDEA   I have recaptured now my crown and throne,   115
   My brother and my father; Colchians hold
   The golden fleece; my kingdom is won back;
   My lost virginity returns to me!
   O gods at last appeased! Glad nuptial day!
   Go, finished is the crime. Not yet complete   120
   Is vengeance, finish while thy hand is strong
   To smite. Why stay, why hesitate, my soul?
   Thou art able! All thine anger falls to nought!
   I do repent of that which I have done!
   What hast thou done, O miserable one?   125
   What, miserable? Though I should repent,
   'Tis done, great joy fills my unwilling heart,
   And, lo, the joy increases. But one thing
   Before was lacking—Jason did not see!
   All that he has not seen I count as lost.   130

---

[91] One of the Furies, the avenging goddesses.

JASON She threatens from the roof; let fire be brought,
     That she may perish burned with her own flame.
MEDEA Pile high the funeral pyre of thy sons,
     And rear their tomb. To Creon and thy wife
     I have already paid the honors due.   135
     This son is dead, and this one too shall die,
     And thou shalt see him perish.
JASON   By the gods,
     By our sad flight together, and the bond
     I have not willingly forsaken, spare   140
     Our son! If there is any crime, 'tis mine;
     Put me to death, strike down the guilty one.
MEDEA There where thou askest mercy, and canst feel
     The sting, I thrust the sword. Go, Jason, seek
     The virgin bride; desert a mother's bed.   145
JASON Let one suffice for vengeance.
MEDEA   Had it been
     That one could satisfy my hands with blood,
     I had slain none. Although I should slay two,
     The number is too small for my revenge.   150
JASON Then go, fill up the measure of thy crime,
     I ask for nothing but that thou should'st make
     A speedy end.
MEDEA   Now, grief, take slow revenge;
     It is my day; haste not, let me enjoy. (*Kills the other child*)   155
JASON Slay me, mine enemy!
MEDEA   Dost thou implore
     My pity? It is well! I am avenged.
     O vengeance, no more offerings can I give,
     Nothing is left to immolate to thee!   160
     Look up, ungrateful Jason, recognize
     Thy wife; so I am wont to flee. The way
     Lies open through the skies; two dragons bend
     Their necks, submissive to the yoke. I go
     In my swift car through heaven. Take thy sons!   165
          (*She casts down to him the bodies of her children, and is
               borne away in a chariot drawn by dragons*)
JASON Go through the skies sublime, and in thy flight
     Prove that where thou art borne there are no gods.

Christian Liturgical Drama:
The Mystery Play in France

The Mystery of Adam (12th century) is the earliest extant mystery play. Chiefly in Norman-French, it also contains enough Latin to suggest that it was probably produced during the period when the liturgical drama was passing from the clergy to the laity. Its unusual union of several episodes suggests that it combines several kinds of liturgical action, while its highly explicit stage directions indicate clearly that it was performed at stations near a church, probably on a church porch.

Selected Bibliography

Urwin, K., "*Mystère d' Adam:* Two Problems," *Modern Language Review,* XXXIV (1939), 70–72.

Kaske, R. E., "The Character *'Figura'* in *Le Mystère d' Adam*," in *Medieval Studies in Honor of Urban Holmes,* Chapel Hill, N.C., 1965, pp. 103–110.

THE MYSTERY OF ADAM

Anonymous

Translated by Edward Noble Stone

Characters

DIVINE FIGURE

ADAM

EVE

THE DEVIL

A TROUP OF DEMONS

AN ANGEL

CAIN

ABEL

Prophets: ABRAHAM, MOSES, AARON,

DAVID, SOLOMON, BALAAM, DANIEL,

HABAKKUK, JEREMIAH, ISAIAS

A JEW

NEBUCHADNEZZAR AND HIS MINISTERS

Let Paradise be set up in a somewhat lofty place; let there be put about it curtains and silken hangings, at such an height that those persons who shall be in Paradise can be seen from the shoulders upward; let there be planted there sweet-smelling flowers and foliage; let divers trees be therein, and fruits hanging upon them, so that it may seem a most delectable place.

Then let the Saviour come, clothed in a dalmatic,* and let ADAM *and* EVE *be set before him. Let* ADAM *be clothed in a red tunic;* EVE, *however, in a woman's garment of white, and a white silken wimple; and let them both stand before the* FIGURE; *but* ADAM *a little nearer, with composed countenance;* EVE *however with countenance a little more subdued.*

And let ADAM *himself be well instructed when he shall make his answers, lest in answering he be either too swift or too slow. Let not only* ADAM, *but all the persons, be so instructed that they shall speak composedly and shall use such gestures as become the matter whereof they are speaking; and in uttering the verses, let them neither add a syllable nor take away, but let them pronounce all clearly; and let those things that are to be said be said in their due order.*

Whoever shall speak the name of Paradise, let him look back at it and point it out with his hand.

Then let the Lesson begin: "In the beginning God created the heaven and the earth."

---

* *Dalmatic:* A loose outer garment with short, wide sleeves and open sides, worn by priests at pontifical Mass.

And after this is ended let the choir sing: "And the Lord God formed man."
And when this is ended, let the FIGURE *say:* Adam! *And let him answer:* Lord!

FIGURE   Out of earthly clay   5
    I fashioned thee.

ADAM   I know it, yea!

FIGURE   A living soul to thee I gave,
    In thee my likeness did I grave,
    Mine earthly image making thee.   10
    Never must thou rebellious be.

ADAM   Not I! but I will trust thee aye,
    And my Creator I'll obey.

FIGURE   A fitting fere* I've given thee
    (Eve is she hight) thy wife to be—   15
    Thy wife to be and partner,
    And thou must ever cleave to her
    Do thou love her, let her love thee;
    So shall ye both be blest of me.
    Let her thine own commands obey,   20
    And both be subject to my sway.
    From thy rib-bone her form I wrought;
    No stranger she, but from thee brought.
    Out of thy body I shaped her frame;
    From thee, not from without, she came.   25
    Govern her, then, with counsel wise,
    Nor let dissent betwixt you rise,
    But love and mutual service great.
    Such is the law of wedlock's state.

FIGURE (*To* EVE)   Now will I speak to thee, O Eve.   30
    Take heed, nor lightly this receive:
    If thou to do my will art fain,
    Thy heart its goodness will retain;
    Honor and love to me accord,
    Thy Maker and acknowledged Lord;   35
    To serve me by thy heart inclined
    With all thy might and all thy mind.
    Love Adam, hold him dear as life;
    He is thy husband, thou his wife;
    Ever to him submit thy heart   40
    And from his teaching ne'er depart;
    Serve him and love, with willing mind;
    Therein is wedlock's law defined.
    If thou art proved a helper meet,
    I'll set you both in glory's seat.   45

EVE   Lord, I will do what pleaseth thee,
    In nothing will neglectful be;
    To thee, as sovereign, I will bow,

¹⁴ Mate.

And him my fere and liege avow.
To him I will at all times cleave,   50
From me good counsel he'll receive;
Thy pleasure and his service aye
Will I perform, in every way.

(*Then let the* FIGURE *call* ADAM *nearer, and more particularly
addressing him, say*)   55

   Listen! O Adam. Hearken unto me.
I formed thee; now this gift I add in fee;
Thou mayest live alway—if you loyal be—
And hale and sound, from every sickness free.

   Thou'lt hunger not, nor thirst shall thee annoy,   60
Neither shall heat nor cold thine ease destroy,
Nor weariness thy perfect bliss alloy,
Nor any suffering abate thy joy.

   All of thy life in pleasance thou shalt spend;
'T will not be short—a life withouten end!   65
I tell thee this, and will that Eve attend;
Unless she heed, to folly she will bend.

   Dominion over all the earth ye'll hold;
Birds, beasts—all creatures—be by you controlled;
Who grudgeth this, his worth is lightly told,   70
For your demesne shall the whole world enfold.

   Of good and ill I grant you choice to make;
(Who hath such choice is tethered to no stake;)
Weigh all in the balance fairly, nor mistake;
Be true to me, my counsel ne'er forsake.   75

   Leave thou the evil, choose the good as guide;
Love thou thy Lord, and keep thee at his side;
None other counsel e'er for mine be tried:
Do this, so shalt thou without sin abide.

ADAM   Great thanks I give thee for thy kindness, Lord,   80
Who madest me and dost such grace accord,
To place both good and evil in my ward.
Thy service shall my fullest joy afford.

Thou art my Lord, and in myself I see
Thy handiwork, for thou didst fashion me;   85
Nor ever shall my will so stubborn be,
But that my chiefest care be serving thee.

(*Then let the* FIGURE *with its hand point out Paradise to* ADAM, *saying*)
Adam!

ADAM   Lord!   90
FIGURE   Hear my plan; lift up thine eyes;
   This garden see.
ADAM   Its name?
FIGURE   'Tis Paradise.
ADAM   A place most fair!   95

FIGURE   Myself did it devise
   And plant. Who here shall dwell as friend I'll prize.
   I place it in thy trust, to keep for aye.
                 (*Then shall he send them into Paradise, saying*)
   I set you both herein.   100
ADAM   And shall we stay?
FIGURE   Through all your life. Nothing shall you affray;
   Now ye can neither die nor waste away.
               (*Let the choir sing:* "And the Lord took the man."
     Then shall the FIGURE *stretch forth his hand toward Paradise, saying*)   105
   The nature of this garden I'll recite:
   Here shalt thou feel the lack of no delight;
   No earthly good, desired of any wight,
   But each may here be found in measure right.
   Here wife from man shall no harsh word obtain,   110
   Nor man from wife have shame or cause to plain;
   Begetting, man shall sinless still remain,
   And woman bear her children without pain. For aye thou'lt live; so
      blest is this sojourn,
   With passing years thine age no change shall learn;   115
   Nor dread of death shall bring to thee concern;
   I will thy dwelling here to be eterne.
             (*Let the choir sing:* "And the Lord said unto ADAM."
      Then let the FIGURE *with his hand point out unto* ADAM *the trees of
                            Paradise, saying*)   120
   Of all these fruits thou mayest eat each day.
          (*And let him show him the forbidden tree, and its fruits, saying*)
   This I forbid thee, here make no essay;
   If thou dost eat thereof thou'rt dead straightway;
   My love thou'lt lose, thy weal with woe repay.   125
ADAM   All thy commandments will I keep in mind,
   Nor I nor Eve to break them be inclined;
   If for one fruit such dwelling were resigned,
   Rightly should I be outcast to the wind. If for an apple I thy love gainsay,
   Ne'er in my life can I my folly pay;   130
   A traitor should judgèd be for aye,
   Who doth himself forswear, his lord betray.
   (*Then let the* FIGURE *go to the church, and let* ADAM *and* EVE *walk about,
   innocently delighting themselves in Paradise. In the mean time, let the demons
   run to and fro through the square, making fitting gestures; and let them come,*   135
   one after another, alongside of Paradise, showing EVE *the forbidden fruit, as if
   entreating her to eat thereof. Then let the* DEVIL *come unto* ADAM; *and he shall
                            say unto him*)
DEVIL   How liv'st thou, Adam?
ADAM   In felicity.   140
DEVIL   Is it well with thee?
ADAM   There's nothing vexeth me.

DEVIL	It can be better.
ADAM	Nay—I know not how.
DEVIL	Then, wouldst thou know?
ADAM	It recks* me little now.
DEVIL	I know, forsooth!
ADAM	What boots it me to learn?
DEVIL	And why not, pray?
ADAM	Naught doth it me concern.
DEVIL	Concern thee 't will!
ADAM	I know not when.
DEVIL	I'll not make haste to tell thee, then.
ADAM	Nay, tell me!
DEVIL	No! I'll keep thee waiting

Till thou art sick of supplicating.

ADAM	To know this thing I have no need.
DEVIL	Thou dost deserve no boon, indeed!

The boon thou hast thou canst not use.

ADAM	Prithee, how's that?
DEVIL	Thou'lt not refuse

To hear? Well, then,—'twixt thee and me,—

ADAM	I'll listen, most assuredly!
DEVIL	Now mark me, Adam. I tell thee it

For thine own good.

ADAM	That I'll admit.
DEVIL	Thou'lt trust me, then?
ADAM	Full trust I bring!
DEVIL	In every point?
ADAM	All—save one thing.
DEVIL	What thing is that?
ADAM	This: I'll do naught

Offensive to my Maker's thought.

DEVIL	Dost fear him so?
ADAM	I fear him; yes—

Both love and fear.

DEVIL	That's foolishness!

What can he do thee?

ADAM	Good and bale.
DEVIL	Thou'st listened to an idle tale!

An evil thing befall thee? Why,
In glory born, thou canst not die!

ADAM   God saith I'll die, without redress,
Whene'er his precepts I transgress.

DEVIL   What is this great transgression, pray?
I fain would learn without delay.

ADAM   I'll tell thee all in perfect truth.
This the command he gave, forsooth:

[146] Concerns.

145
150
155
160
165
170
175
180
185

Of all the fruits of Paradise
I've leave to eat (such his advice)—   190
—All, save one only, which is banned;
That I'll not touch, e'en with my hand.

DEVIL   Which fruit is that?

(*Then let* ADAM *stretch forth his hand and show him the forbidden fruit,*
saying)   195

ADAM   See'st yonder tree?
That fruit hath he forbidden me.

DEVIL   Dost know the reason?

ADAM   Certes, no!

DEVIL   The occasion of this thing I'll show: 200
No whit cares he for all the rest;
But yon, that hangeth loftiest,
—The fruit of Knowledge—can bestow
The gift all mysteries to know.
If thou eat'st that, 't will profit thee.   205

ADAM   In what way, pray?

DEVIL   That thou shalt see:
Thine eyes will straightway be unsealed,
All future things to thee revealed;
All that thou will'st thou canst perform;   210
'T will bring thee blessings in a swarm.
Eat, and thou shalt repent it not;
Then thou'lt not fear thy God, in aught;
Instead, thou'lt be in all his peer;
For this, he filled thy soul with fear.   215
Wilt trust me? Then to taste proceed.

ADAM   That will I not!

DEVIL   Fine words, indeed!
Thou wilt not?

ADAM   No!   220

DEVIL   A fool art thou!
Thou'lt yet mind what I tell thee now.

(*Then let the* DEVIL *depart; and he shall go to the other demons, and he*
shall make an excursion through the square; and after some little interval,
cheerful and rejoicing, he shall return to his tempting of ADAM, *and he shall say*   225
unto him)

How farest thou, Adam? Wilt change thy mind?
Or still to stubbornness inclined?
I meant to tell thee recently
God as his almsman* keepeth thee.   230
He put thee here the fruit to eat;
Hast other recreation sweet?

ADAM   Here nothing lacks I could desire.

DEVIL   Dost to naught loftier aspire?

230 Dependent.

Canst boast thyself a man of price!   235
—God's gardener of Paradise!
He made thee keeper of his park;
Wilt thou not seek a higher mark?
Filling thy belly!—Surely, he
Had nobler aims in mind for thee!   240
Listen now, Adam, and attend
The honest counsel that I lend:
Thou couldest from thy Lord be free,
And thy Creator's equal be.
In brief, I'll this assurance make: 245
If of this apple thou partake, (*Then shall he lift his hand toward Paradise*)
Then thou shalt reign in majesty!
In power, God's partner thou canst be!

ADAM   Go! Get thee hence!

DEVIL   What! Adam. —How!   250

ADAM   Go! Get thee hence! Satan art thou!
Ill counsel giv'st thou.

DEVIL   How, pray tell!

ADAM   Thou would'st deliver me to hell!
Thou would'st me with my Lord embroil,   255
Move me from bliss to bale and moil.
I will not trust thee! Get theee hence!
Nor ever have the impudence
Again to come before my face!
Traitor forsworn, withouten grace!   260

(*Then shall the* DEVIL, *sadly and with downcast countenance, depart from*
ADAM *and he shall go even unto the gates of Hell, and he shall hold converse
there with the other demons. Thereafter, he shall make an excursion among the
people; but presently he shall draw near to Paradise, on the side where* EVE *is and
approaching* EVE *with a cheerful countenance and much blandishment, he*   265
                    thus accosteth her)

DEVIL   Eve, hither am I come, to thee.

EVE   And prithee, Satan, why to me?

DEVIL   Seeking thy weal, thine honour, too.

EVE   God grant it!   270

DEVIL   Then, thy fears eschew.
Long since, I've mastered by my pains
Each secret Paradise contains;
A part of them to thee I'll tell

EVE   Begin, then, and I'll listen well.   275

DEVIL   Thou'lt hearken to me?

EVE   Hearken?—yea,
Nor vex thy soul in any way.

DEVIL   Thou'lt keep it hidden?

EVE   Yea, in truth.   280

DEVIL   Nor publish it?

EVE	Not I! forsooth.
DEVIL	Then, to this contract I'll agree,
	Nor further pledge require of thee.
EVE	Might'st safely trust my promise, though.
DEVIL	Thou'st been to a good school, I trow!
	Adam I've seen—a fool is he.
EVE	A little hard.
DEVIL	He'll softer be;
	But harder now than iron is.
EVE	A noble man!
DEVIL	A churl! I wis.*
	Thought for himself he will not take;
	Let him have care, e'en for thy sake.
	Thou art a delicate, tender thing,
	Thou'rt fresher than the rose in spring;
	Thou'rt whiter than the crystal pale,
	Than snow that falls in the icy vale.
	An ill-matched pair did God create!
	Too tender thou, too hard thy mate.
	But thou'rt the wiser, I confess;
	Thy heart is full of cleverness;
	Therefore 't is good to treat with thee.
	To thee I'd speak; have faith in me.
	Let none know of it.
EVE	Who should know?
DEVIL	Not Adam even.
EVE	Be it so.
DEVIL	Now will I speak; do thou give ear.
	None, save us twain, is present here,
	(And Adam yon, who hath not heard.)
EVE	Speak up! He'll not perceive a word.
DEVIL	I'll shew thee, then, what crafty plot
	Was 'gainst you in this garden wrought:
	The fruit God gave you to possess
	Hath in it little godliness,
	But in the fruit to you forbidden
	Exceeding virtue lieth hidden;
	Therein is found of life the dower,
	Dominion, mastery, and power,
	Knowledge of evil and of good.
EVE	What savour hath 't?
DEVIL	'T is heavenly food!
	To thy fair body, to thy face,
	Most meet it were to add this grace:
	That thou be queen of the world—of this,

285
290
295
300
305
310
315
320
325

292 Think.

84 ANONYMOUS

Of the firmament, and of the abyss—
And know all things that shall befall,
And be the mistress of them all.

EVE   Is such the fruit?   330

DEVIL   Truly, it is.

(*Then shall* EVE *carefully consider the forbidden fruit, and after she hath considered it for a season, she shall say*)

EVE   Only to see it brings me bliss!

DEVIL   But what, if thou shalt eat it, Eve?   335

EVE   How should I know?

DEVIL   Wilt not believe?
First take it, and to Adam bear;
Heaven's crown will then be yours to wear;
Ye shall be like your Maker then,   340
He'll hide no secrets from your ken.
Soon as ye've eaten of the fruit,
Your hearts it straightway will transmute;
With God ye'll be—free from all blight—
Of equal goodness, equal might.   345
Come taste it!

EVE   That I'm thinking on.

DEVIL   Trust Adam not!

EVE   I'll taste anon.

DEVIL   But when?   350

EVE   Let me deferment make
Till Adam his repose shall take.

DEVIL   But eat it. Put thy fears away.
'Twere childish greatly to delay.

(*Then shall the* DEVIL *depart from* EVE *and shall go unto Hell; but* ADAM *shall* 355 *come unto* EVE, *being sore displeased because the* DEVIL *hath spoken with her, and he shall say unto her*)

ADAM   Say, wife, what thing of thee inquired
That evil Satan?—what desired?

EVE   'T was of our honour he conversed.   360

ADAM   Believe him not— the traitor curs'd!
That he's a traitor, I've no doubt.

EVE   And wherefore, pray?

ADAM   I've found him out.

EVE   What boots it? See him once—thou'lt find   365
Eftsoons* he'll make thee change thy mind!

ADAM   Not he! I'll trust him not at all
Till I've made trial of him withal.
Let him no more come near to thee;
He's full of foulest perfidy,   370
His sovereign Lord he sought to cheat

---

366 Immediately afterward.

And set himself in the highest seat.
A knave that's done such wickedness
To thee shall never have access.

(Then a serpent, cunningly put together, shall ascend along the trunk of the for- 375
bidden tree, unto which EVE *shall approach her ear, as if hearkening unto its*
counsel. Thereafter, EVE *shall take the apple, and shall offer it unto* ADAM.
But he shall not yet receive it, and EVE *shall say unto him)*

EVE Eat! Adam; thou know'st not what is offered!
    Let's take the gift thus freely proffered. 380

ADAM Is it so good?

EVE   That thou shalt see;
    But canst not, till it tasted be.

ADAM I fear!

EVE   Then, leave it! 385

ADAM Nay, I'll taste.

EVE Faint-heart! so long thy time to waste!

ADAM I'll take the fruit.

EVE   Here, eat it! So
    Thou shalt both good and evil know. 390
    But, first, myself I'll taste it now.

ADAM And I next?

EVE   Marry! Next shalt thou.

    (Then shall EVE *eat a part of the apple, and she shall say unto* ADAM)
    I've tasted! Pardi! What a savour! 395
    I've never known so sweet a flavour!
    With such a savour 't is endued—

ADAM What savour?

EVE   —as no mortal food!
    Now do mine eyes so clearly see 400
    I seem Almighty God to be!
    All that has been or shall befall
    I know—am mistress of it all!
    Eat! Adam, eat! No more abstain;
    Thou'lt do it to thy lasting gain. 405

    (Then shall ADAM *receive the apple from the hand of* EVE, *saying)*

ADAM I'll trust thy word, thou art my peer.

EVE Take, eat; thou hast no cause to fear.

    (Then shall ADAM *eat a part of the apple; and having eaten it, he shall straight-*
    way take knowledge of his sin; and he shall bow himself down so that he cannot be 410
    seen of the people, and shall put off his goodly garments, and shall put on poor
    garments of fig-leaves sewn together; and manifesting exceeding great sorrow, he
    shall begin his lamentation)

ADAM O! sinful wretch! What have I done?
    Now my avoidless death's begun! 415
    Now, without rescue, am I dead;
    My fortune fair is evil sped;
    My lot, a little time ago

So happy, now is turned to woe;
I my Creator did forsake 420
Through counsel of my evil make.
O! sinner lost! What shall I do?
How can I now my Maker view?
Upon my Maker can I look,
Whom through my folly I forsook? 425
Ne'er such ill bargain did I strike!
Now do I know what sin is like!
O Death! Why dost thou let me live,
Nor to the earth clean riddance give?
Why, cumbering earth, do I yet stay? 430
The depths of hell must I essay;
In hell my dwelling aye shall be
Until one come to succour me.
In hell henceforward I shall fare,
And whence shall help come to me there? 435
Whence shall aid thither come to me?
Who from such pains shall set me free?
Why did I thus my Lord offend?
Now there is none can be my friend;
None will there be can me avail; 440
Lost am I now, withouten fail!
Against my Lord I've done such sin,
No suit with him can I begin,
For right is he, and wrong am I.
O God! 'Neath what a curse I lie! 445
Who, henceforth, will take thought of me,
Who've wronged the King of Majesty?
'Gainst Heaven's own king such wrong I've done
That claim upon him have I none.
No friend I have, no neighbour near, 450
Who as my surety might appear;
And whom shall I beseech for aid,
When mine own wife hath me betrayed,
Whom God gave me my fere to be?
An evil counsel gave she me! 455
Alas! O Eve!
(*Then shall he look upon* EVE, *his wife, and shall say*)
Insensate wife!
In an ill hour I gave thee life!
O had that rib been burned, alas! 460
That brought me to this evil pass!
Had but the fire that rib consumed,
That me to such confusion doomed!
Why, when from me the rib he drew,
Burned he it not, nor me then slew? 465

The rib the body hath betrayed,
Ill-treated, and all useless made.
I know not what to say or try;
Unless grace reach me from on high,
From pain I cannot be released, 470
Such malady on me hath seized.
Alas! O Eve! Woe worth the day—
Such torment holdeth me in sway—
Thou e'er becamest wife to me!
Now I am lost through heeding thee; 475
Through heeding thee I'm in this plight,
Brought down most low from a great height.
Thence will no mortal rescue me—
None, save the God of majesty.
What say I? Wretch! Why named I him? 480
He helped? I've gained his anger grim!
None will e'er bring me succour—none
Save him who'll come as Mary's son.
From none can I henceforth get aid
Since we our trust with God betrayed. 485
Then, let all be as God ordains;
No course, except to die, remains.
          (*Then let the choir begin:* "The voice of the Lord God walking
                              in the garden."
After this hath been sung, the FIGURE *shall come, wearing a stole, and looking* 490
about him, as if seeking to know where ADAM *is. But* ADAM *and* EVE *shall be*
hidden in a corner of Paradise, as if conscious of their wretchedness; and the FIG-
                    URE *shall say:* Adam, where art thou?
Then shall they both arise and stand before the FIGURE, *yet not fully upright, but*
through shame for their sin, bending forward a little, and exceeding sad; and let 495
                    ADAM *make answer*)
ADAM   Lord, I'm here.
I hid; thine anger did I fear;
I saw my nakedness revealed,
Therefore myself have I concealed. 500
FIGURE   What hast thou done? Why blushest thou?
Who thee from goodness drew away?
What hast thou done? Why blushest thou?
How shall I reckon with thee now?
Thou hadst, a little while ago, 505
No reason any shame to show;
Now see I thee downcast, distraught;
Small joy thy dwelling here hath brought!
ADAM   So great is my confusion, I
Do hide me from thee, Lord. 510
FIGURE   And why?
ADAM   Such shame my body doth enlace,

I dare not look thee in the face.

FIGURE   Why overstept'st thou my decree?
Hath this brought any gain to thee?   515
My servant thou, thy Lord am I.

ADAM   This can I in no wise deny.

FIGURE   In mine own likeness thee I wrought,
Why set'st thou my command at naught?
After mine image formed I thee;   520
Why hast thou thus affronted me?
Thou did'st in no wise heed my hest;*
Deliberately thou hast transgressed!
That fruit thou atest which I said
I had for thee prohibited.   525
Didst reckon thus my peer to be?
I do not think thou'lt jest with me!
(*Then shall* ADAM *stretch forth his hand toward the* FIGURE, *and thereafter
toward* EVE, *saying*)

ADAM   The woman that thou gavest me,   530
She first did this iniquity;
She gave me it, and I did eat;
Now is my life with woe replete.
Most rashly meddled I therein;
'T was through my wife that I did sin.   535

FIGURE   Thy wife thou trustedst more than me,
Didst eat without my warranty;
This recompense to thee I'll make:
Curs'd shall the ground be for thy sake,
Where thou shalt wish thy grain to sow,   540
Nor shall it any fruit bestow;
Curs'd shall it 'neath thy hand remain,
And all thy tillage be in vain.
Its fruit to thee it shall not yield,
But thorns and thistles fill thy field;   545
'T will change whate'er is sown by thee;
Its curse shall be thy penalty.
With grievous toil and bitter pain
To eat thy bread shalt thou be fain;
In sweat, in great affliction, aye   550
Thou'lt live hereafter, night and day.
(*Then shall the* FIGURE *turn toward* EVE, *and with a threatening countenance
shall say unto her*)

FIGURE   Thou, too, O Eve, a woman of sin,
Didst thy rebellion soon begin   555
And briefly heededest my decree.

EVE   The wicked serpent tempted me.

FIGURE   Didst think through him to be my peer?

522 Command.

Hast learned to make things hidden clear?
Erstwhile thou heldest sovereignty   560
Over all living things that be;
How quickly hast thou lost thy crown!
Now see I thee sad and cast down.
Hast thou thereby got gain or hurt?
I'll render thee thy just desert;   565
Thy service I will thus repay:
Woe thee shall find in every way;
In sorrow thou'lt thy children bear,
In pain throughout their life they'll fare;
In sorrow they'll be born of thee,   570
And end their days in misery.
To such distress and direful need
Thou'st brought thyself and all thy seed;
All thy descendants ever more
Thy sin shall bitterly deplore.   575

(And EVE *shall make answer, saying)*

EVE Yea, I have sinned—'t was through my folly vain;
For one sole apple I have got such bane
As doometh me and mine to bitter pain—
Great toll of wretchedness, with little gain!   580
If I have sinned, 't was nothing strange, I fear,
Whenas the serpent charmed my silly ear;
Much guile he hath, no lamb doth he appear;
Unhappy he who would his counsel hear!
I took the fruit—'t was folly, now I see;   585
This wickedness I wrought 'gainst thy decree;
I tasted it, and won thine enmity.
For a little fruit, my life must forfeit be!

(Then shall the FIGURE *threaten the serpent, saying)*

FIGURE Thou, too, O Serpent, curs'd shalt be;   590
I will exact my due of thee:
Upon thy belly shalt thou go
Through all the days thy life shall know;
The dust shall be thy daily food,
On moor or heath, or in the wood;   595
Woman shall bear thee enmity,
An evil neighbour ever be;
To strike her heel thou'lt lie in wait,
But she herself shall bruise thy pate;
Thy head with such a Hammer smite   600
'T will put thee in a sorry plight;
Therefrom shall she such aidance get,
She'll be avengèd of thee yet!
Thou sought'st her acquaintance to thy woe;
She yet shall bring thy head full low;   605

There yet shall spring from her a Root
That all thy cunning shall confute.
> (*Then shall the* FIGURE *drive them forth out of Paradise, saying*)

FIGURE From Paradise, go! get you hence!
Ye've made ill change of residence. 610
On earth shall ye your dwelling make;
In Paradise ye have no stake,
No title there, and no concern;
Forth shall ye go, without return.
Through judgment ye can claim naught there; 615
Now find you lodgement otherwhere.
Go! From felicity depart!
Hunger shall fail you not, nor smart,
But pain and weariness abound
Day after day, the whole week round. 620
On earth a weary term ye'll spend,
And die thereafter, in the end;
After ye've tasted death, straightway
To hell ye'll come without delay.
Here exile shall your bodies quell, 625
And danger daunt your souls in hell.
Satan shall hold your souls in thrall;
There'll be no helper ye can call,
None by whom rescue can be sent,
Unless I pity and relent. 630
> (*Let the choir sing:* "In the sweat of thy face."
> *In the meantime there shall come an angel, clad in white garments, and bearing
> a shining sword in his hand, whom the* FIGURE *shall set over against the gate of
> Paradise, and he shall say unto him*)

FIGURE Guard well my Paradise, that ne'er 635
Again this outlaw enter there—
That him no leave or chance befall
To touch the fruit of Life at all;
With this thy sword that flameth aye,
Forever bar for him the way. 640
> (*When they shall be clean outside of Paradise, sad and confounded in appearance,
> they shall bow themselves to the ground, even unto their feet, and the* FIGURE
> *shall point to them with his hand, his face being turned toward Paradise; and
> the choir shall begin:* "Behold Adam is become as one (of us)."
> *And when this is ended, the* FIGURE *shall go back unto the church.* 645
> *Then shall* ADAM *have a spade, and* EVE *a mattock, and they shall begin to
> till the ground, and they shall sow wheat therein. After they shall have finished
> their sowing, they shall go and sit for a season in a certain place, as if wearied
> with their toil, and with tearful eyes shall they look back ofttimes at Paradise,
> beating their breasts. Meanwhile shall the* DEVIL *come and plant thorns and* 650
> *thistles in their tillage, and then he shall depart. When* ADAM *and* EVE *shall
> come to their tillage, and when they shall have beheld the thorns and thistles that*

have sprung up, stricken with grievous sorrow, they shall cast themselves down *upon the ground; and remaining there, they shall beat their breasts and their* *thighs, manifesting their grief by their gestures; and* ADAM *shall then begin his* 655 *lamentation*)

ADAM   Woe worth the hour—hateful for ever more—
That e'er my sinfulness so whelmed me o'er!
That I forsook the Lord whom all adore!
To succour me, whom shall I now implore? 660
(*Here let* ADAM *look back at Paradise; and he shall lift up both hands toward* *it; and devoutly bowing his head, he shall say*)
O Paradise! How sweet to dwell in thee!
Garden of glory! Oh how fair to see!
Thence, for my sin, must I an outcast be; 665
Hope of return is ever lost to me!
I was therein; but little joy I got;
Through heeding counsel false I thence was brought.
Now I repent; scorn earn I, as I ought.
'T is all too late, my sighing boots me naught. 670
Where was my memory? whither fled my wit?
That I, for Satan, glory's King should quit!
Now, sore my grief—no help is there in it;
My sin on history's pages shall be writ.
(*Then shall* ADAM *lift up his hand against* EVE, *who shall have been set some* 675 *little distance away, on higher ground, and moving his head with great indig-* *nation, he shall say unto her*)
O evil woman, full of perfidy!
How quickly to perdition brought'st thou me,
When thou mad'st sense and reason both to flee! 680
Now I repent, but can no pardon see.
To evil how inclined wert thou to cleave!
How quick the serpent's counsel to receive!
Through thee I die, through thee my life I leave.
Writ in the book thy sin shall be, O Eve! 685
Seest thou these tokens of confusion dread?
Earth doth perceive what curse o'erhangs our head;
'T was corn* we sowed—thistles spring up instead.
Greatly we've sweat, ill have we profited!
   Thou seest the outset of our evil state; 690
Great sorrow 't is, but greater doth await;
To hell shall we be brought, without rebate;
Pain shall not fail us, neither torment great.
   O wretched Eve! How seemeth it to thee?
This hast thou gained thee as thy dowery: 695
Ne'er more canst thou bring man felicity,
But aye opposed to reason thou wilt be.

688 Wheat.

All they who come hereafter, of our seed,
Shall feel the punishment of thy misdeed;
Thou sinnedst; all must bear the doom decreed.
Late will he come who shall relieve their need.

(*Then let* EVE *make answer unto* ADAM)

EVE Adam, dear lord, much hast thou chidden me,
And much reviled and blamed my villainy;
If I have sinned, my punishment I dree;*
Guilty I am, of God I'll judgèd be.

Toward God and thee much evil have I wrought;
'Gainst my offence long shall reproach be brought;
My fault is great, my sin torments my thought!
O wretched me! Of good in me is naught!

No ground have I wherewith to make my plea,
That God's just doom be not pronounced on me;
Forgive me!—no atonement can I see,
Else would my sacrifice be offered free.

A miserable sinner, vile within,
Hiding my face from God for my great sin—
Oh, take me. Death! Now let my death begin!
Shipwrecked and lost, the shore I cannot win.

The serpent fell, the snake of evil fame,
Caused me to eat the apple, to my shame;
I gave it thee—to serve thee was mine aim;
For this thy sin thyself I may not blame.

Oh, why did I my Maker's will defy?
Wherefore, dear lord, thy teachings thus deny?
Thou sinnedst, but the root thereof am I!
Our sickness doth a long, long cure imply.

For my great error, my adventure vain,
Our seed, henceforth, will dearly pay again;
The fruit was sweet, bitter will be the pain!
In sin we ate, ours will the guilt remain.

Yet, nonetheless, my hope in God I base:
Sometime atonement will our guilt efface,
And I shall know God's favour and his grace;
His power will bring us from that evil place.

(*Then shall the* DEVIL *come, and three or four other devils with him, bearing in their hands chains and iron shackles, which they shall place on the necks of* ADAM *and* EVE.

And certain ones shall push them on, others shall drag them toward hell; other devils, however, shall be close beside hell, waiting for them as they come, and these shall make a great dancing and jubilation over their destruction; and other devils shall, one after another, point to them as they come; and they shall take them up and thrust them into hell; and thereupon they shall cause a great smoke to arise,

---

705 Endure.

*and they shall shout one to another in hell, greatly rejoicing; and they shall dash
together their pots and kettles, so that they may be heard without. And after some
little interval, the devils shall go forth, and shall run to and fro in the square;* 745
certain of them, however, shall remain behind in hell)

(*Then shall come* CAIN *and* ABEL. *Let* CAIN *be clad in red garments, but* ABEL
*in garments of white; and they shall till the ground that hath been made ready;
and after* ABEL *shall have rested a little from his labor, let him address his brother*
CAIN *in a fond and friendly fashion, saying unto him*) 750

ABEL   O Cain, my brother, of one blood are we;
     Both Adam's sons—the first of men was he—
     And of one mother, also—Eve hight she;
     In serving God, let us no niggards be.
       To do our Maker's hests let us be fain; 755
     So serve him that we shall his love regain,
     Which our poor parents lost through folly vain.
     Let steadfast love abide betwixt us twain.
       So serve we God that we may please him aye,
     Pay him his dues in full, keep naught away; 760
     If we with cheerful hearts his word obey,
     No dread of death our souls shall e'er affray.
       Pay we his tithes,* his tributes justly tell,
     First-fruits and offerings, sacrifice as well;
     If ever greed do us to fraud impel, 765
     Without remission we'll be lost in hell.
       Betwixt us twain let great affection be,
     Let never envy come, nor enmity;
     For why should strife arise 'twixt thee and me,
     When all the earth to us hath been made free? 770
(*Then shall* CAIN *look at his brother* ABEL, *as if mocking him; and he shall say
unto him*)

CAIN   Good brother Abel, featly* canst thou preach!
     Canst order well thy points, and stablish each;
     But should one practice that which thou dost teach, 775
     In a few days, his gifts their end would reach!
       This giving tithes ne'er suited me one whit.
     Thou, with thy stuff, thy pious vows acquit,
     And I, with mine, will do what seems me fit;
     If I do wrong, thou'lt not be damned for it! 780
       To love each other, Nature taught us twain;
     Let neither, then, dissemble aught, or feign;
     Whiche'er of us shall raise contention vain,
     Let him pay dear and have good cause to plain.
(*Let* ABEL *again address his brother* CAIN; *since* CAIN *hath answered him more* 785
mildly than is his wont, he shall say)

---

763 A small part, usually a tenth, of one's yearly production, paid as tax.
773 Gracefully.

ABEL	Good brother Cain, now list to me.	
CAIN	Gladly! Pray tell what moveth thee.	
ABEL	Thine own advantage.	
CAIN	Better still!	790
ABEL	Rebel no more against God's will,	
	Nor flaunt thy froward hardihood:	
	This I adjure thee.	
CAIN	Well and good!	
ABEL	Then let us sacrifice, that thus	795
	The Lord may be well pleased with us;	
	If his forgiveness thus we win,	
	He will no more regard our sin,	
	Nor heaviness our souls shall touch;	
	To gain his love doth profit much.	800
	Come, let us on his altar set	
	Such gifts as shall his favour get;	
	Let us his love beseech, and pray	
	That he defend us night and day.	

(*Then shall* CAIN *make answer, as if* ABEL'S *counsel were acceptable to him,* 805 *saying*)

CAIN	Good brother, thou hast said aright!	
	This sermon didst thou well indite,*	
	And I will pay good heed to it;	
	Let's make our offerings, as is fit.	810
	What offerest thou?	
ABEL	A lamb I'll bring,	
	The fairest and the choicest thing	
	That I can find in all the fold;	
	That one I'll offer, nor withhold;	815
	And incense, also, will I bring.	
	Now I have told thee everything;	
	What offerest thou?	
CAIN	Wheat from my field,	
	Such as God suffereth it to yield.	820
ABEL	The choicest?	
CAIN	God forbid! Instead,	
	From that, tonight I'll make my bread.	
ABEL	Such sacrifice will not avail	
	To please him.	825
CAIN	Pish! a silly tale!	
ABEL	Thou'rt a rich man, much cattle hast—	
CAIN	That have I!	
ABEL	Count them, to the last,	
	And give to him a tenth of all;	830
	This part shalt thou God's portion call.	
	Offer him this whole-heartedly,	

808 Express.

And rich reward shall come to thee.
Wilt do this?

CAIN   Fie! Thou'rt mad, I guess!   835
To give a tenth were foolishness;
Of ten, there'd then be left but nine!
A fig for all thy counsel fine!
Come, let each offer severally
What seems him good.   840

ABEL   So let it be.

(*Then shall they go unto two great stones, which shall have been made ready for
this purpose. The one stone shall be set at such a distance from the other that, when
the* FIGURE *appeareth,* ABEL'S *stone shall be on his right hand, but the stone of*
CAIN *on his left,* ABEL *shall offer up a lamb, and incense, whence he shall cause*   845
smoke to arise. CAIN *shall offer a handful of corn. Then the* FIGURE *shall appear,*
and he shall bless ABEL'S *offering, but the offering of* CAIN *shall he regard with*
scorn. Wherefore, after the oblation, CAIN *shall set his face against* ABEL; *and*
when their sacrifices are ended, they shall go again unto their own places.
Then shall CAIN *come unto* ABEL, *seeking craftily to lead him forth, that he may*   850
slay him; and he shall say unto him)

CAIN   Good brother, let us hence! Arise!
ABEL   Wherefore?
CAIN   Ourselves to exercise,
To view the tillage of our fields,   855
What growth, what flowering it yields;
Then, to the meadows we will go,
Thereby we'll be refreshed, I know.
ABEL   I'll go with thee, where thou shalt say.
CAIN   Come then; it will thy pains repay.   860
ABEL   Thou art my elder brother, thou,
And to thy wishes I will bow.
CAIN   Do thou go first, I'll follow thee
With loitering steps and leisurely.

(*Then shall they both go to a place apart, and secret, as it were, where* CAIN   865
shall rush upon ABEL, *like unto a mad man, desiring to slay him; and he shall*
say unto him)

CAIN   Abel, thou diest!
ABEL   Wherefore? Speak!
CAIN   I will my vengeance on thee wreak!   870
ABEL   Have I thee wronged?
CAIN   Aye, wronged enow!
A traitor fully proved art thou.
ABEL   Surely I'm not!
CAIN   Dost thou deny?   875
ABEL   I'd ne'er do treachery—not I!
CAIN   Thou hast already!
ABEL   How? I'd know.

CAIN   Thou'lt know full soon.

ABEL   Can this be so!   880

CAIN   I'll set thee right full speedily.

ABEL   But thou canst nothing prove 'gainst me.

CAIN   The proof's here!

ABEL   God will overthrow it.

CAIN   I'll slay thee!   885

ABEL   God will surely know it.

    (*Then shall* CAIN *lift up his right hand threateningly against him, saying*)

CAIN   Lo, this is what will prove the case!

ABEL   In God alone my trust I place.

CAIN   'Gainst me, small aid from him thou'lt get.   890

ABEL   Haply, he'll thwart thy purpose yet.

CAIN   He cannot turn thy death aside.

ABEL   By his good pleasure I abide.

CAIN   Would'st hear wherefore I will thee kill?

ABEL   O tell me it!   895

CAIN   Tell thee I will.
    Too long hast thou usurped God's ear!
    Through thee, my prayers he would not hear,
    Through thee, he spurned the gifts I bore;
    Dost think I'll not pay off this score?   900
    Certes, I'll render thee thy pay!
    Dead on this sand thou'lt lie today!

ABEL   If thou slay me, great wrong 't will be;
    God will avenge my death on thee.
    God wot I thee have harmèd not,   905
    Nor slandered thee to him in aught;
    But bade thee so thy acts employ
    That thou his favor might'st enjoy,
    Bade thee grant all his claims—such things
    As tithes, firstfruits, and offerings;   910
    Thereby hadst thou his love obtained;
    Through failing this, his wrath thou'st gained.
    God keepeth faith; who serves him fain,
    Shall nothing lose, but greatly gain.

CAIN   Thou'st talked too long; thou diest now!   915

ABEL   Brother! what say'st? My guide wert thou;
    Hither I came in perfect trust.

CAIN   Trust cannot save thee; die thou must!
    I'll slay thee now! I challenge thee!

ABEL   May God be merciful to me!   920

    (*Then shall* ABEL *kneel down, facing the East; and he shall have a pot hidden
    underneath his garments, which* CAIN *shall strike violently, as if he were slaying*
    ABEL *himself.* ABEL, *however, shall lie stretched out, as if he were dead.
    The choir shall sing:* "Where is Abel, thy brother?")

Meanwhile, the FIGURE *shall come forth from the church and go toward* CAIN, 925
and after the choir shall have ended the responsorium,* he shall say unto CAIN,
as if very wroth with him)

FIGURE   Where is thy brother Abel, Cain?
To make rebellion art thou fain?
'Gainst me hast thou begun to strive? 930
Show me thy brother now, alive!

CAIN   How should I know where he may be?
—At home, or with his husbandry?
And why should I be forced to find him?
I was not set to keep and mind him! 935

FIGURE   What hast thou done with him, O Cain?
Right well I know! Him thou hast slain!
Thy brother's blood to me doth cry;
Its voice hath come to me on high.
Great wickedness didst thou commit, 940
Thy life long thou'lt be curs'd for it;
This malison* thou'lt bear for aye;
As was the deed, so be the pay!
Yet I will not that thou be slain,
But pass thy life in dole and pain; 945
Whoever, therefore, Cain shall slay,
A sevenfold penalty shall pay.
Thou slewest him who trusted me;
Most heavy shall thy penance be.

(*Then shall the* FIGURE *return unto the church; but the devils shall come forth* 950
and lead CAIN *away to hell, beating him again and again.* ABEL, *also, shall they*
lead away, albeit in a more gentle fashion)

(*Then shall the Prophets be made ready, one by one, in a secret place, as their*
order is.
Let the Lesson be read in the choir. "*You, I say, do I challenge, O Jews.*" 955
And let the Prophets be summoned by name; and when they shall come forward,
let them advance with dignity and utter their prophecies loudly and distinctly.
So shall ABRAHAM *come first, an old man with an exceeding long beard, ar-*
rayed in ample robes; and when he shall have sat for a brief season upon the
bench, let him begin his prophecy in a loud voice) 960

ABRAHAM   Thy seed shall possess the gates of their enemies, and in thy seed
shall all the nations of the earth be blessed.
Abraham, I; such is my name.
Hear, now, the message I proclaim:
Whose hope is on God's promise stayed, 965
Let him keep faith and trust unswayed;
Whose faith is fixed in God, for aye
Will God be with him. This I say

---

926 A series of responses sung by a choir and a soloist, singing alternately.
942 Curse.

Through knowledge; God my faith did test;
I did his will, obeyed his hest; 970
For him, mine own son had I slain,
But God's hand did my hand restrain.
The unfinished offering did he bless,
'T was counted me for righteousness.
God promised me—'t is truth, indeed,— 975
An heir shall issue from my seed
Who shall subdue his every foe,
And strong and mighty shall he grow;
Their gates possessing, ne'er shall he
A menial in their castles be. 980
E'en such an one, sprung from my root,
Shall all our punishment commute;
By him the world shall ransomed be,
And Adam from his pain set free;
And men, of every race and kind 985
On earth, through him shall blessing find.

(*After these words have been said, and a little time hath intervened, the devils
shall lead* ABRAHAM *to hell.*

Then shall come MOSES, *bearing in his right hand a rod, and in his left the
tables* (*of stone*). *After he hath seated himself, let him utter his prophecy*) 990

MOSES God shall raise up a prophet from among your brethren, to him shall ye
hearken as to me.

That which I speak, through God I saw;
From our own brethren, from our law,
God shall raise up a man who'll be 995
Prophet and sum of prophecy.
Heaven's secrets all shall he receive;
Him, more than me, shall ye believe.

(*Thereafter shall he be led away by the* DEVIL *into hell. In like manner shall it be
done with all the prophets.* 1000

Then shall come AARON, *in the vestments of a bishop, bearing in his hand a rod
having flowers and fruit; and being seated, let him say*)

AARON From this rod* the flower that springeth
Perfume of salvation bringeth;
Sweet its fruit, 't will end all crying 1005
And all sorrow for our dying.
This rod—unplanted, without root,—
Can bud, and blossom, and bear fruit;
Such Rod from mine own line shall spring
And deadly hurt to Satan bring. 1010
No taint of fleshly birth he'll bear,
Yet man's own nature shall he wear.
This is salvation's fruit, 't will free
Adam from his captivity.

1003 Aaron's rod was used to perform miracles and is held to be the first of the bishops' staffs.

(After him, let DAVID *draw nigh, arrayed in royal robes and wearing a crown;* 1015
and let him say)

DAVID   Truth is sprung out of the earth; and justice hath looked down from
heaven. For the Lord will give goodness; and our earth shall yield her fruit.
Out of the earth shall truth arise,
And justice watch us from the skies;   1020
Yea, God shall give us all things good;
Our land shall richly bring us food,
Her increase yield that saving Bread
Whereby Eve's sons shall all be fed;
O'er all the earth shall he hold sway,   1025
Shall stablish peace, drive war away.
(Thereafter let SOLOMON *come forth, with the same adornments as* DAVID, *yet
in such a manner that he shall seem to be younger; and sitting down, let him say)*

SOLOMON   Being ministers of God's kingdom, you have not judged rightly,
nor kept the law of justice, nor walked according to the will of God;   1030
horribly and speedily will he appear to you; for a most severe judgment shall
be for them that bear rule. For to him that is little, mercy is granted.
God gave to you his law, O Jews,
But faith with him ye would not use;
Wardens of his domain were ye,   1035
He stablished you right royally;
Ye would not render judgment right,
Your verdicts were in God's despite;
His will ye would perform no more,
And your iniquity waxed sore.   1040
Your deeds shall all to light be brought;
Most grievous vengeance shall be wrought
On those that highest sat of all.
And they shall suffer fearful fall.
But God shall set the lowly free   1045
And raise him to felicity.
This saying shall be verified
When God's own Son for us hath died.
The masters of the law 't will be
That slay him, most unlawfully;   1050
Against all justice, all belief,
They'll crucify him, like a thief.
But they shall lose their lordly seat,
Who envy him, and ill entreat.
Low down they'll come, from a great height,   1055
Well may they mourn their woeful plight.
Howbeit, poor Adam shall he see
And pity, and from sin set free.
(After him shall come BALAAM, *an old man arrayed in ample robes, sitting upon
an ass; and he shall come into the midst, and still sitting upon his beast he shall* 1060
speak his prophecy)

BALAAM A Star shall rise out of Jacob, and a Sceptre shall spring up from
     Israel, and shall strike the chiefs of Moab, and shall waste all the children
     of Seth.

     From Jacob shall a Star arise,   1065
     Reddening with heaven's own fire the skies,
     A Sceptre spring from Israel
     That shall 'gainst Moab's rule rebel,
     Their haughtiness diminishing;
     For out of Israel Christ shall spring,   1070
     And he shall be that glorious Star
     Whereby all things illumined are,
     His faithful ones he'll lead to joy,
     But all his enemies destroy.

     (*Thereafter shall* DANIEL *draw nigh, in years a youth, but in his demeanour like* 1075
     unto an old man; and when he shall have seated himself, let him speak his proph-
          ecy, stretching forth his hand against those whom he addresseth)

DANIEL When the Most Holy One shall have come, your anointing shall
     cease.

     You, O ye Jews, do I address,   1080
     Who use toward God great wickedness.
     When he, the Chief of Saints, draws near,
     Then your confusion shall appear,
     For then shall your anointing cease;
     All claim thereto must ye release.   1085
     This Holy One is Christ, 't is plain;
     Through him the faithful life shall gain.
     To earth come, for his people's sake,
     On him your race great war shall make,
     Shall drive him to his Passion; so   1090
     Shall they their unction's grace forego,
     Thenceforth nor priest nor king shall own,
     Their Law lost through themselves alone.

     (*After him shall come* HABAKKUK, *an old man; and sitting down, when he be-*
     ginneth his prophecy, he shall lift up his hands toward the church, manifesting 1095
                    wonder and fear. Let him say)

HABAKKUK O Lord, I have heard thy speech and was afraid. In the midst of the
     two beasts shalt thou be recognized.

     From God strange tidings have I heard,
     Whereby my mind is greatly stirred;   1100
     So long did I this sign explore
     My heart thereat is troubled sore:
     Between two beasts shall he be shown,
     By all the world he shall be known.
     To him of whom this thing I say,   1105
     Behold, a star shall point the way;
     Shepherds shall find him, thither brought,
     Within a crib in dry stone wrought

Wherefrom the beasts shall eat their hay;
To kings he'll be declared straightway;   1110
Thither the star shall lead the kings,
All three shall bring their offerings.

(*Then shall* JEREMIAH *enter, bearing a scroll in his hand; and let him say*)

JEREMIAH   Hear ye the word of the Lord, all ye men of Judah, that enter in at
these gates to adore the Lord. Thus saith the Lord of Hosts, the God of   1115
Israel: Make your ways and your doings good, and I will dwell with you in
this place.

The holy word of God now hear,
All who are of his school, give ear,
All righteous Judah's mighty race,   1120
Who in his household have a place:
Ye all shall enter by this door,
Our Lord to worship, evermore;
The Lord of Hosts to you doth cry,
The God of Israel, from on high: 1125
Make good your ways, amend each one,
Let them be straight as furrows run,
And let your hearts be clean, withal,
Lest any evil you befall;
Let all your thoughts in good abound,   1130
Nor wickedness therein be found.
If thus ye do, then God will come.
And in your dwellings make his home,
The Son of God, the glorious,
For you come down to earth, and thus,   1135
As mortal man, with you shall be—
The Lord of heavenly majesty!
Adam he shall from prison bring,
Himself as ransom offering.

(*After him shall come* ISAIAS, *bearing a book in his hand, and wrapped in a*   1140
large mantle; and let him speak his prophecy)

ISAIAS   And there shall come forth a rod out of the root of Jesse, and a flower
shall rise up out of his root, and the Spirit of the Lord shall rest upon it.

Now will I tell a wondrous thing:
From Jesse's root a Rod shall spring,   1145
Shall burgeon and bear flower withal,
Whereto great honor shall befall;
The Holy Spirit shall enclose
This flower, and shall thereon repose.

(*Then shall there stand up a certain one of the synagogue, disputing with* ISAIAS;   1150
and he shall say unto him)

JEW   Now, Sir Isaias, answer me:
Is this a tale, or prophecy?
This thing thou'st told—pray, what is it?
Didst it invent, or is it writ?   1155

Thou'st been asleep—didst dream the rest?
Speak'st thou in earnest, or in jest?
ISAIAS   This is no tale, 't is very truth!
JEW   Then, let's know all of it, forsooth!
ISAIAS   What I have spoke is prophecy.   1160
JEW   Writ in a book?
ISAIAS   Yea, verily.
   —In Life's! I've dreamed it not, but seen!
JEW   And how?
ISAIAS   Through grace of God, I ween.   1165
JEW   Thou seem'st to me a dotard grey.
   Thy mind and sense all gone astray!
   A soothsayer thou seem'st, indeed,
   Skilled in the glass, perchance, to read;
   Come, read me now this hand, and tell   1170
               (*Then shall he show him his hand*)
   Whether my heart be sick or well.
ISAIAS   Thou hast sin's murrain* in thy soul,
   Ne'er in thy life shalt thou be whole!
JEW   Am I, then, sick?   1175
ISAIAS   With error sore.
JEW   When shall I mend me?
ISAIAS   Never more!
JEW   Begin thy soothsaying, I pray.
ISAIAS   There'll be no lie in what I say.   1180
JEW   Come now, re-tell thy vision, quick!
   If 't was a rod, or but a stick,
   And what its blossom shall engender;
   Then due respect to thee we'll render,
   And all the present generation   1185
   Will listen to thy dissertation.
ISAIAS   Then, this great marvel shall ye hear;
   —Such ne'er was told to mortal ear,
   To such a marvel never man
   Hath listened since the world began: 1190
   "Behold, a virgin shall conceive and bear a son, and his name shall be called
      Emmanuel."
   The time is near, within your ken,
   Not tarrying or distant, when
   A virgin shall conceive, most fair,   1195
   And, virgin still, a son shall bear;
   His name shall be Emmanuel.
   Saint Gabriel shall the message tell;
   The maid shall Virgin Mary be,
   She'll bear the fruit of Life's own tree,   1200
   Jesus, our Saviour, who shall bring

¹¹⁷³ Pestilence.

Adam from dole and suffering,
And him to Paradise return.
That which I speak from God I learn;
And this shall surely be fulfilled,   1205
And ye thereon your hope shall build.
(*Then shall come* NEBUCHADNEZZAR, *adorned as befitteth a king. And he
shall say*)

NEBUCHADNEZZAR   Did we not cast three youths, bound, into the fire?
HIS MINISTERS   True, O King.   1210
NEBUCHADNEZZAR   Lo, I see four men loose, walking in the midst of the fire,
and they have no hurt, and the form of the fourth is like the Son of God.
Hear now a wondrous prodigy,
Unheard-of by all men that be!
This saw I with the children three   1215
Cast in the blazing fire by me:
The fire was hot and fierce to dree,
The bright flame glowed exceedingly;
The three rejoiced and made great glee,
Within the furnace walking free.   1220
But when I came the fourth to see,
(Great comfort to the rest gave he,)
His face shone, full of majesty,
The Son of God he seemed to be!*

1224 The ms. breaks off at this point, probably very near the end of the play [translator's note].

Christian Liturgical Drama:
The Mystery Play in England

THE TRIAL OF JOSEPH AND MARY *(15th century) is one of
forty-two plays comprising the* Ludus Coventriae *cycle of
mystery plays. Unlike the York and Chester cycles, this cycle
seems to have had no particular connection with the city of
Coventry, and may, in fact, have been the property of a troupe
of strolling players. The extant manuscript contains the heading
"N. Town Cycle." The "N." is thought to be an abbreviation
for the Latin word* nomen, *or "name," and is interpreted to
mean any name which the company wished to insert before the
play title. The plays were often presented, as reflected in this
modernized version, on a series of stages or stations; the audience
(and sometimes the actors) moved to each as the action required.
The cycle is notable for its emphasis on New Testament materials,
and this play illustrates the high order of theatricality achieved by a
relatively simple, straightforward exploitation of a single episode
from the Bible story.*

Selected Bibliography

Chambers, E. K., *The Medieval Stage* (Oxford, 1903), II, 416–422.

Clark, T. B., "A Theory Concerning the Identity and History of the Ludus
Conventriae Cycle of Mystery Plays," *Philological Quarterly,* XII
(1933), 144–169.

Deasy, C. P., *St. Joseph in the English Mystery Plays,* Washington, D.C.,
1937.

Fry, Timothy, "The Unity of Ludus Coventriae," *Studies in Philology,*
XLVIII (1951), 527–570.

Swenson, E. L., *Inquiry into the Composition and Structure of the Ludus
Coventriae,* Minneapolis, 1914.

Thompson, E. N. S., "The Ludus Coventriae," Modern Language Notes,
XXI (1906), 18–20.

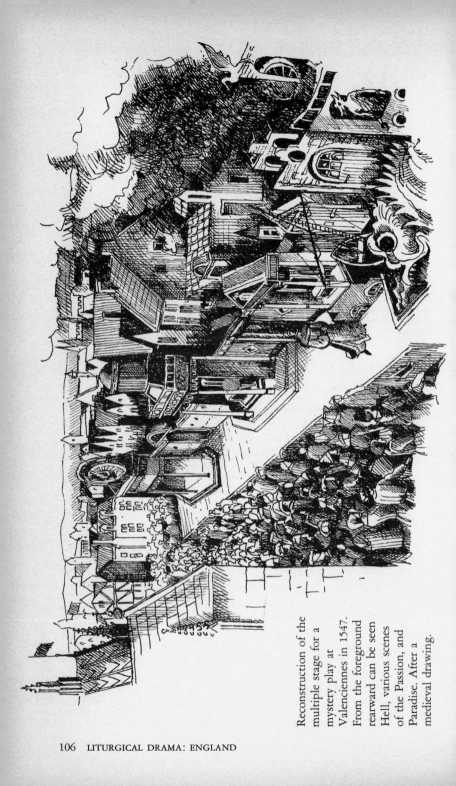

Reconstruction of the multiple stage for a mystery play at Valenciennes in 1547. From the foreground rearward can be seen Hell, various scenes of the Passion, and Paradise. After a medieval drawing.

THE TRIAL OF
JOSEPH AND MARY

Anonymous

Modernized version by Barry B. Adams

Characters

SUMMONER
RAISE-SLANDER
BACKBITER
BISHOP ABIZACHAR
FIRST DOCTOR *of the Law*
SECOND DOCTOR *of the Law*
MARY
JOSEPH

Prologue

(SUMMONER* *addresses the audience as* BISHOP ABIZACHAR *and the two*
        DOCTORS OF THE LAW *proceed to their station*)

SUMMONER   Make way, sirs, and let my lord the bishop come
   And sit in the court, the laws for to do.
   And I shall go through this place them for to summon
   That be in my book: to court they must come, too.

   I warn you here all about   5
   When I summon you, all the rout,
   Look ye fail for no doubt
        at the court to appear.
   Both John Jordan and Geoffrey Gyle,
   Malkyn Milksoak and fair Mabel,   10
   Stephen Sturdy and Jack-at-the-style,
        and Sandy Saddler;

   Tom Tinker and Beatrice Bell,
   Piers Potter and Watt-at-the-well,
   Sim Smallfaith and Katey Kell,   15
        and Bartholomew the butcher;
   Kit Cackler and Colette Crane,
   Gill Neatly and fair Jane,

Summoner: formerly, an official who served court summonses.

Paul Pewterer and Pernel Prane,
   and Phillip the good fletcher;   20

Colin Crane and Davy Drydust,
Lucy Liar and Letty Littletrust,
Miles the miller and Colley Crackcrust,
   both Betty the baker and Robin Red.
And look ye ring well in your purse   25
For else your cause may speed the worse,
Though ye should sling God's curse
   even at my head.

Both Bonnie the browster and Sibyl Sling,
Madge Merryweather and Sabina Spring,   30
Tiffany Twinkle-ear fail for no thing:
   the court shall meet today.
               (SUMMONER *retires to the Bishop's station*)

Scene

               (RAISE-SLANDER *enters and addresses the audience*)
RAISE-SLANDER   Hail, sirs, God save you all!   35
   Here is a fair people, I must say!
   Good sirs, can tell what men me call?
   I think ye can not, by this day.
   Yet I walk wide and by many a way,
   And wherever I come I do no good.   40
   To raise slander is all my lay.*
   Backbiter is my brother of blood.
   Has anyone seen him here today?
   I wish to God that he were here!
   And by my truth I dare well say   45
   That if we twain together appear
   More slander we two shall up rear
   Within an hour throughout this town
   Than ever there was this thousand year,
   Or else I shrew* you, both up and down!   50
               (*Enter* BACKBITER)
   Now by my truth I have a sight
   Even of my brother. See, here he is.
   Welcome dear brother! My troth I plight;
   Your gentle mouth let me now kiss.   55
BACKBITER   Gramercy, brother, so have I bliss.
   I am full glad we've met this day.

   ⁴¹ Song.
   ⁵⁰ Curse.

108   ANONYMOUS

RAISE-SLANDER   Right so am I, brother, iwis,*
    Much gladder than I can say.
    But yet, good brother, I you pray,   60
    Tell all these people what is your name.
    For if they knew it, my life I lay,
    They would you worship and spread your fame.
BACKBITER   I am Backbiter that spoileth all game,
    Both known and felt in many a place.   65
RAISE-SLANDER   By my truth, I said the same!
    And yet some did wish for you ill grace.
BACKBITER   But hark, Raise-slander, canst thou aught tell
    Of any new thing that was done of late?
RAISE-SLANDER   Within a short while a thing befell—   70
    I know thou will laugh right well thereat!
    For in truth a handsome harvest of hate
    (If it were known) thereof will grow.
BACKBITER   If I may raise therewith debate
    I shall not spare the seed to sow.   75
RAISE-SLANDER   Sir, in the temple a maid there was
    Called Maid Mary, the truth to tell.
    She seemed so holy within that place
    Men said she was fed by a holy angel.
    She made a vow with man never to dwell   80
    But to live as a chaste and clean virgin.
    However it be, her womb doth swell
    And now is as great as thine or mine.
BACKBITER   Hah! That old shrew Joseph, my troth I plight,
    Was so enamoured of that young maid   85
    That of her beauty when he had sight
    He ceased not til he had her assayed.
RAISE-SLANDER   Ah, nay, nay! Much worse she hath him paid!
    Some fresh young gallant she loveth much more,
    And he his legs to hers hath laid—   90
    And that doth grieve the old man sore!
BACKBITER   By my truth, that may well be,
    For fresh and fair she is to sight;
    And such a morsel, it seems to me,
    Would bring a young man much delight.   95
RAISE-SLANDER   Such young damsels of beauty bright
    And of shape so comely also
    Of their tails oft times are light
    And right ticklish under the toe.
BACKBITER   That old cuckold was well beguiled   100
    To that fresh woman when he was wed;
    Now must he father another man's child,
    And with his sweat it shall be fed.

[58] Assuredly.

RAISE-SLANDER A young man may do more cheer in bed
To a fresh young wench than may an old.   105
That is the cause, as I have read,
That many a man is a cockelwold.*
(*Here* BISHOP ABIZACHAR, *sitting between the two doctors of the law and hearing
                    this slander, calls the detractors to him.*)

BISHOP Hark, ye fellows, why speak ye such shame   110
Of that good virgin, fair maid Mary?
Ye be accursed her so to defame—
She that is of life so good and holy.
Of her to speak such villainy
Ye put my heart in a heavy mood.   115
I charge you cease from your false cry,
For she is kin, of my own blood.

BACKBITER What care I though that she be?
All great with child her womb doth swell.
Go call her hither: thy self shall see   120
That it is truth that I thee tell.

RAISE-SLANDER Sir, for your sake I shall keep council;
To grieve you, sir, I am right loath.
But list, sirs, list what sayeth the bell:
Now great with child our fair maid goeth.   125

FIRST DOCTOR Take good heed, sirs, what ye do say.
Advise you well what ye present.
If this be found false another day,
Full sore ye shall your tale repent.

BACKBITER Sir, the maid, as you say, is good and gent,*   130
Both comely and gay—indeed, a fair wench;
And perhaps with help she would consent
To set a cuckhold on the high bench.

BISHOP This heavy tale my heart doth move—
Of her to hear such dalliance.   135
If she should merit such reproof
She shall sore rue her governance.
Sim Summoner! In haste wend thou thy way.
Bid Joseph and his wife by name
At the court appear this day,   140
Themselves to purge of their ill fame.
Say that I hear of them great shame
Which causes me great heaviness.
If they be clean and without blame,
Bid them come hither and show witness.   145

SUMMONER All ready, sir! I shall them call,
Here at your court they will appear.
And if I may them meet withal,

---

[107] Cuckolded.
[130] Refined.

I hope right soon they shall be here.

(SUMMONER *forces his way through the audience on his way to the station of* 150
JOSEPH *and* MARY)

Make way, there, sirs! Let me come through!
A man of worship here comes in place!
Of courteous men there be too few.
Put off your hoods, with an evil grace! 155
Do me some worship before my face,
Or, by my soul, I shall you make!
If I must bowl you down in my race,
For fear I shall make your asses quake!
But yet some money I'll gladly take, 160
And then withdraw my great rough toe:
Gold or silver I never forsake,
But ever do as all summoners do. (*He approaches* JOSEPH *and* MARY)
Hark, Joseph, with thy fair spouse!
My lord the bishop for you hath sent. 165
To him it is told that in thy house
A cuckold's bow is each night bent—
Who shoots the bolt is like to be shent!*
Fair maid, that tale ye can best tell!
Now, by your troth, you know what is meant: 170
Did not the archer please you well?

MARY   Of God in heaven I take witness
That sinful deed was never my thought.
I am still a maid of pure cleanness,
As I was when into this world brought. 175

SUMMONER   No other witness need be sought:
That thou art with child, each man may see.
I charge you both ye tarry not,
But to the bishop come forth with me.

JOSEPH   To the bishop with you we'll wend; 180
Of our purgation we have no doubt.

MARY   Almighty God shall be our friend,
And then the truth shall be found out.

SUMMONER   Yea! In this wise excuses her every scout
When her foul sin doth her defame. 185
But lowly then they begin to lout*
When they be guilty and found to blame.
Therefore come forth, old cuckold by name;
The bishop shall your ways expose.
Come forth also, my goodly dame, 190
A clean housewife, as I suppose!
I shall you tell—no need to gloze—*

168 To come to harm.
186 Bow down.
192 To fawn or flatter.

If ye were mine and had this knack,
I would each day beshrew your nose
If ye had brought me such a pack! (*They proceed to the bishop's station.*)   195
My lord the bishop! Here have I brought
This goodly couple at your own bidding.
It seems to me she is so fraught,
A lullaby sweet she soon must sing.

RAISE-SLANDER   If you had her a cradle brought   200
You might have helped to ease her purse;
Because she is your cousin, sir,
I pray she will not fare the worse!

BISHOP   Alas, Mary, what hast thou wrought?
Great shame I feel for thy own sake.   205
How hast thou changed thy holy thought?
Did that old Joseph with strength thee take?
Or hast thou chosen another mate
By whom thou art thus brought to shame?
How art thou come into this state?   210
How hast thou lost thy holy name?

MARY   My name I hope is safe and clean:
God may witness I am a maid.
Of fleshly lust or other sin
In deed nor thought I never assayed.   215

FIRST DOCTOR   How should thy womb thus be arrayed,
So greatly swollen as it is?
Unless some man thee overlaid
Thy womb should never grow thus, iwis.

SECOND DOCTOR   Hark thou, Joseph, I am afraid   220
That thou hast wrought this open sin;
This woman thou hast thus betrayed
With great flattering or some false gin.*

BACKBITER   Now, by my truth, ye hit the pin!
With that conclusion, in faith, I hold.   225
Tell us now how thou didst her win,
Or acknowledge thyself a cockelwold!

JOSEPH   She is to me a true clean maid,
And I to her am clean also.
Of fleshly sin I never assayed   230
Since that time we two were wed.

BISHOP   Thou shalt not scape from us yet so;
First thou shalt tell us another lay.
Straight to the altar thou shalt go,
The drink of vengeaunce there to assay.   235
Here is the bottle of God's vengeance:
This drink shall be now thy purgation.

223 Device.

This hath such virtue through God's ordinance,
That whoever shall drink of this potation
And goes, indeed, in short procession   240
Here in this place the altar about,
If he be guilty of maculation*
Plain in his face shall it shine out.
If thou be guilty, tell us; let see:
Against God's might be not too bold.   245
If thou presume and guilty be,
God thou dost grieve many a fold.

JOSEPH   I am not guilty, as I first told.
    Almighty God I take to witness.

BISHOP   Now take this drink which here I hold,   250
    And then proceed, or else confess.

        (*Here* JOSEPH *drinks and goes about the altar seven times*)

JOSEPH   This drink I take with meek intent.
    As I am guiltless to God I pray:
    Lord, as thou art omnipotent,   255
    In me show then the truth this day.
    About this altar I make my way.
    O gracious God, help thy servant!
    As I am guiltless against yon maid,
    Thy hand of mercy this time me grant.   260

SUMMONER   This old shrew may not well go;
    Long he tarryeth to go about.
    Lift up thy feet, set forth thy toe,
    Or by my truth thou gettest a clout!

BACKBITER   Now, sir, bad luck come to thy snout!   265
    What aileth thy legs now to be lame?
    Thou didst them put right freshly out
    When thou didst play with yon young dame.

RAISE-SLANDER   I pray to God—give him mischance!
    Here his legs do fold with age,   270
    But with this damsel when he did dance
    This same old churl had enough courage!

JOSEPH   Ah, gracious God, help me this tide
    Against these people that me defame;
    As I have never touched her side,   275
    Now safeguard me from worldly shame.
    About this altar to keep my fame
    Seven times have I gone round about.
    If I be worthy to suffer blame,
    O God, now let my sin shine out.   280

BISHOP   Now Joseph, give thanks to God thy lord
    Whose high mercy doth thee excuse.

242 Staining or making impure.

For thy purgation we shall record;
To sin with her thou didst never muse.*
But Mary, thyself may not refuse.   285
All great with child we see thee stand.
What kind of man did thee misuse?
Why hast thou sinned against thy husband?

MARY   I trespassed never with earthly wight;
Therefore I hope by God's own hand   290
Here to be purged before your sight—
From all sin clean, as is my husband.
Give me the bottle here where I stand,
And here shall I drink before your face;
About the altar, by your command,   295
Seven times I'll go, begging God's grace.

FIRST DOCTOR   See how this bold creature would presume
Against the high God to test her might!
Though God's vengeance her should consume
She will not reveal her false delight.   300
Thou art with child we see in sight;
To us thy womb doth thee accuse.
There was never yet woman in such a plight
That from mankind could her excuse.

RAISE-SLANDER   In faith, I suppose this woman slept   305
Without any cover while it did snow,
And a flake by chance into her mouth crept
And thereof the child in her womb doth grow!

BACKBITER   Then beware, dame, for this I well know:
When it is born if the sun should burn   310
It will turn to water, as I trow,
For snow unto water doth ever return.

SECOND DOCTOR   With God's high might look thou not jape;*
Of thy purgation well thee advise.
If thou be guilty thou may not 'scape.   315
Beware of God and His assize.*

MARY   I trust in His grace I shall never Him grieve.
His servant I am in word, deed and thought.
A maid undefiled I hope He'll me prove.
I pray you, therefore, hinder me not.   320

BISHOP   Now by that good Lord that all this world hath wrought,
If God on thee show any kind of token,
Purgation I trow was never so dear bought
Or holy faith so unwisely broken.
Hold here the bottle and take a large draught,   325
And about the altar make thy procession.

284 Think.
313 Jest.
316 Court.

MARY Thy help, O Lord, I have besought,
And now I drink of this potation.
> (*Here the Blessed Virgin drinks and then goes about the altar*)
God, as I never knew of man's maculation, 330
But ever have lived in true virginity,
Send me this day thy holy consolation
That all this fair people my cleanness may see.
O gracious God, as thou didst choose me
To be thy mother, of me to be born, 335
Save thy tabernacle that clean is kept for thee,
Who now am put to reproof and scorn.
Gabriel me told with words from on high
That you of your goodness would become my child.
Help now of your kindness, my plea not deny. 340
Ah, dear son, I pray you help your mother mild!

BISHOP Almighty God, what may this mean?
For all this drink of God's potation
This woman with child is fair and clean,
Without foul spot or maculation. 345
I cannot by my calculation
Prove her guilty and sinful of life;
It appeareth openly by her purgation,
She is a clean maid, both mother and wife.

RAISE-SLANDER By my father's soul, here is great guile! 350
Because she is one of your own kin,
The drink is changed by some false wile,
That she may escape, despite her sin.

BISHOP Because thou deemest that we do wrong,
And for thou didst them first defame, 355
Thou shalt right here before this throng
To show the truth now drink the same.

RAISE-SLANDER Sir, in good faith, one draught I'll pull,
If these two drinkers have not all spent.
> (*Here he drinks, and feeling a pain in his head he falls down*) 360
Out, out, alas! What aileth my skull!
My head with fire it seems is brent.*
Mercy, good Mary, I now repent
Of my cursed speech and false outrage.

MARY May the Lord of heaven omnipotent, 365
Of His great mercy your sickness assuage.

BISHOP We all on knees fall here to ground,
Thou God's hand-maid praying for grace.
Our cursed language with shame here crowned,
Good Mary forgive us here in this place. 370

MARY Now God forgive you all your trespass
And also forgive you all defamation—

362 Burned.

All ye have said, both more and less,
To my hindrance and maculation.

BISHOP   Now blessed virgin, we thank you all   375
For your good heart and great patience.
We will go with you home to your hall
To do you service with high reverence.

MARY   I thank you heartily for such benevolence;
But unto your own house I pray you to go,   380
And take these people home with you hence:
I am not disposed to leave this place now.

BISHOP   Then farewell maiden and pure virgin,
Farewell true handmaid of God in bliss.
We all to you lowly incline   385
And take our leave, as right it is.

MARY   Almighty God your ways now bless
For that high Lord is most of might.
May He you speed that ye not miss
In heaven of Him to have a sight.   390

JOSEPH   Honored in heaven by that high lord
Whose endless grace is so abundant
That He doth show the true record
Of every wight that is His true servant.
That lord to worship with heart pleasant   395
We both be bound here in this place,
Who our purgation us did grant
And proved us pure through His high grace.

MARY   In truth, good spouse, I thank him highly
Of His good grace for our purgation.   400
Our cleanness is known full openly
Because of His great consolation.

The Wakefield Master

THE WAKEFIELD SECOND SHEPHERDS' PLAY (c.1475) *is one
of five plays of the Towneley Cycle, a cycle of thirty-two plays,
by the so-called Wakefield Master. Although unidentified, this
writer is credited with having produced the most complex
and sophisticated examples of the mystery play in English.
This, his best known work, illustrates the freest and most
imaginative use of original materials known to this dramatic
type, as well as an effective early use of analogous lines of action.*

Selected Bibliography

Baugh, A. C., "The Mak Story," *Modern Philology*, XV (1918), 729–734.

Cady, F. W., "The Wakefield Group in the Towneley Plays," *Journal of
English and Germanic Philology*, XI (1912), 244–262.

Cosbey, R. C., "The Mak Story and its Folklore Analogues," *Speculum*,
XX (1945), 310–317.

Ross, Lawrence J., "Symbol and Structure in the *Secunda Pastorum*,"
Comparative Drama, I (1967), 122–143.

THE SECOND SHEPHERDS' PLAY

by The Wakefield Master

Modernized version by Anthony Caputi

Characters

FIRST SHEPHERD, COLL
SECOND SHEPHERD, GIB
THIRD SHEPHERD, DAW
MAK
GILL, HIS WIFE
ANGEL
MARY

(*Enter the* FIRST SHEPHERD)

FIRST SHEPHERD   Lord, but it's cold, and I'm wretchedly wrapped.
  My hands nearly numb, so long have I napped.
  My legs creak and fold, my fingers are chapped;
  It is not as I would, for I am all lapped
    In sorrow.   5
  In storms and tempest,
  Now in the east, now in the west,
  Woe is him has never rest
    Midday nor morrow!

  But we poor shepherds that walk on the moor,   10
  We're like, in faith, to be put out of door;
  No wonder, as it stands, if we be poor,
  For the tilth of our lands lies fallow as a floor,
    As ye ken.
  We are so lamed,   15
  So taxed and shamed,
  We are made hand-tamed
    By these gentlery-men.

  Thus they rob us of rest. Our Lady them harry!
  These men that are lord-fast, they make the plough tarry.   20
  Some say it's for the best; but we find it contrary.
  Thus are tenants oppressed, in point to miscarry,
    In life.

Thus hold they us under;
Thus they bring us in blunder.   25
It were a great wonder
    If ever we should thrive.

'Gainst a man with painted sleeves, or a brooch, now-a-days,
Woe to him that shall grieve, or one word gainsay!
No man dare him reprove, what mastery he has.   30
Yet no man believes one word that he says,
    No letter.
He can make purveyance,
With boast and arrogance;
And all is for maintenance   35
    Of men that are greater.

There shall come a swain as proud as a po,*
He must borrow my wain,* and my plough also,
That I am full fain to grant ere he go.
Thus live we in pain, anger, and woe   40
    By night and day.
Whatever he has willed
Must at once be fulfilled.
I were better be killed
    Than once say him nay.   45

It does me good, as I walk round alone,
Of this world for to talk in manner of groan.
To my sheep will I stalk, now as I moan;
There abide on a ridge, or sit on a stone,
    Full soon.   50
For I know, pardie,*
True men if they be,
I'll get more company
    Ere it be noon. (*Moves aside*)
                    (*Enter the* SECOND SHEPHERD)   55
SECOND SHEPHERD   Ben'c'te* and Dominus! What may this bemean?
Why fares this world thus; the like has seldom been.
Lord, the weather is spiteful, and the winds bitter keen,
And the frosts so hideous, they water my een.*
    No lie.   60
Now in dry, now in wet,

---

³⁷ Peacock.
³⁸ Wagon.
⁵¹ *Pardieu:* By God; indeed.
⁵⁶ Benedicte.
⁵⁹ Eyes.

Now in snow, now in sleet,
My shoes freeze to my feet,
   And all is awry.

But as far as I ken, wherever I go,   65
We poor wedded men endure much woe,
Crushed again and again, it falls oft so.
And Silly Capel, our hen, both to and fro
   She cackles;
But begin she to croak,   70
To groan or to choke,
For our cock it's no joke,
   For he's in the shackles.

These men that are wed have never their will.
When they're full hard bestead,* they sigh and keep still.   75
God knows they are led full hard and full ill;
In bower nor in bed say they aught until
   Ebb tide.
My part have I found,
And my lesson is sound: 80
Woe to him that is bound,
   For he must abide.

But now late in our lives—a marvel to me,
That I think my heart rives such wonders to see,
What destiny drives that it should so be—   85
Some men will have two wives, and some men three
   In store.
He has woe that has any;
But so far ken I,
He has moe* that has many,   90
   For he feels sore.

But young men a'wooing, before you've been caught,
Be well ware of wedding, and keep in your thought,
To moan, "Had I known," is a thing that serves naught.
Mickle* mourning has wedding to home often brought,   95
   And griefs,
With many a sharp shower;
You may catch in an hour
What shall seem full sour
   As long as you live.   100

75 Situated.
90 More.
95 Much.

For as ever read I epistle* I've one as my dear,
As sharp as a thistle, as rough as a brere;*
She is browed like a bristle, with a sour lenten cheer;
Had she once wet her whistle, she could sing full clear
   Her paternoster. 105
She's as great as a whale;
She has a gallon of gall;
By him that died for us all
   I would I'd run till I'd lost her.

FIRST SHEPHERD   Gib, look over the row! Full deafly ye stand. 110
SECOND SHEPHERD   Yea, the devil in your maw—ye blow on your hand.
   Saw ye anywhere Daw?
FIRST SHEPHERD   Yea, on a lea-land
   I heard him blow. He comes here at hand,
      Not far. 115
   Stand still.
SECOND SHEPHERD   Why?
FIRST SHEPHERD   I think he comes by.
SECOND SHEPHERD   He'll trick us with a lie
   Unless we beware. 120

(*Enter the* THIRD SHEPHERD, *a boy*)

THIRD SHEPHERD   Christ's cross me speed, and Saint Nicholas!
   Thereof had I need; and it's worse than it was.
   Whoso can take heed and let the world pass;
   It's rank as a weed and brittle as glass, 125
      And slides.
   This world fared never so,
With marvels more and moe,
   Now in weal, now in woe,
      Everything writhes. 130

Never since Noah's flood were such floods seen,
Winds and rains so rude, and storms so keen;
Some stammered, some stood in doubt, as I ween.
Now God turn all to good! I say as I mean,
   Hereunder. 135
These floods so they drown,
Both in fields and in town,
And bear all down,
   They make you wonder.

We that walk in the nights our cattle to keep, 140

---

101 In the New Testament.
102 Briar.

We see queer sights when other men sleep.
Yet methinks my heart lightens; I see my pals peep.
They are two tall wights! Now I'll give my sheep
   A turn.
O full ill am I bent,   145
As I walk on this land,
I may lightly repent,
   If my toes I spurn.

(*To the other two*)   Ah, sir, God you save, and master mine!
A drink would I have, and somewhat to dine.   150
FIRST SHEPHERD   Christ's curse, my knave, thou'rt a lazy swine!
SECOND SHEPHERD   The boy likes to rave! Let him stand there and whine
      Till we've made it.
Ill thrift on thy pate!
Though the fellow came late,   155
Yet is he in state
      To dine—if he had it.

THIRD SHEPHERD   Such servants as I, that sweat and swink,*
Eat our bread full dry, that's what I think.
We're oft wet and weary when master men wink;*   160
Yet come full late both dinners and drink.
   But neatly
Both our dame and our sire,
When we've run in the mire,
Can nip at our hire,   165
   And pay us full lately.

But hear a truth, master, for you the fare make:
I shall do, hereafter, work as I take;
I shall do a little, sir, and between times play.
For I've never had suppers that heavily weigh   170
   In fields.
And why should I bray?
I can still run away.
What sells cheap, men say,
   Never yields.   175

FIRST SHEPHERD   Thou are an ill lad, to ride a-wooing
   With a man that had but little of spending.
SECOND SHEPHERD   Peace, boy! I bade; no more jangling,
   Or I shall make thee afraid, by the Heaven's King,
      With thy frauds.   180
   Where are the sheep, boy; lorn?

158 Toil.
160 Doze.

THIRD SHEPHERD Sir, this same day at morn
   I them left in the corn,
      When they rang lauds.*

   They have pasture good; they cannot go wrong.   185
FIRST SHEPHERD That's right. Oh, by the rood, these nights are long!
   Yet I would, ere we go, let's have us a song.
SECOND SHEPHERD So I thought as I stood, to cheer us along.
THIRD SHEPHERD I grant.
FIRST SHEPHERD The tenor I'll try.   190
SECOND SHEPHERD And I the treble so high.
THIRD SHEPHERD Then the middle am I.
   Let's see how ye chant. (*They sing*)

(*Enter* MAK *with a cloak over his smock*)

MAK Now, Lord, of names seven, that made the moon so pale,   195
   And more stars than I can name; Thy good will fails;
   I am so in a whirl that my jogged brain ails.
   Now would God I were in heaven—where no child wails—
      Heaven so still.
FIRST SHEPHERD Who is it that pipes so poor?   200
MAK God knows what I endure,
   Here a'walking on the moor,
      And not my will!

SECOND SHEPHERD From where do ye come, Mak? What news do ye bring?
THIRD SHEPHERD Is he come? Then everyone take heed to his things. 205
(*Takes the cloak from* MAK)
MAK What! I am a yeoman (hear me you) of the king;
   Make way for me, the Lord's tidings I bring,
      And such.
   Fie on you! Go hence!   210
   This is no pretence.
   I must have reverence.
      And much!

FIRST SHEPHERD Why make ye so quaint, Mak? It's no good to try.
SECOND SHEPHERD Why play ye the saint, Mak? We know that you lie. 215
THIRD SHEPHERD We know you can feint, Mak, and give the devil the lie.
MAK I'll make such complaint, 'lack,* I'll make you all fry
      At a word.
   And tell what ye doth.
FIRST SHEPHERD But, Mak, is that truth?   220
   Go gild that green tooth
      With a turd.

---

184 The early morning service.
217 Alack: an expression of surprise or dismay.

SECOND SHEPHERD   Mak, the devil's in your eye! A stroke would I lend you.
THIRD SHEPHERD   Mak, know ye not me? By God, I could 'tend you.
MAK   God keep you all three! Perhaps I can mend you.   225
    You're a fair company.
FIRST SHEPHERD   Can ye so bend you?
SECOND SHEPHERD   Rascal, jape!*
    Thus late as thou goes,
    What will men suppose?   230
    Sure thou hast an ill nose
      For stealing of sheep.

MAK   And I am true as steel, all men say,
    But a sickness I feel that takes my health away;
    My belly's not well, not at all well today.   235
THIRD SHEPHERD   "Seldom lies the devil dead by the way."
MAK   Therefore
    Full sore am I and ill;
    And I'll lie stone still
    If I've eat even a quill   240
      This month and more.

FIRST SHEPHERD   How fares thy wife? By my hood, tell me true.
MAK   Lies sprawling by the fire, but that's nothing new;
    And a house full of brood. She drinks well, too;
    Come ill or good that she'll always do   245
      But so.
    Eats as fast as she can;
    And each year gives a man
    A hungry bairn* to scan,
      And some years two.   250

    And were I more gracious and richer by far,
    I were eaten still out of house and of barn.
    And just look at her close, if ye come near;
    There is none that knows what 'tis to fear
      Than ken I.   255
    Will ye see what I proffer—
    I'll give all in my coffer
    And masses I'll offer
      To bid her goodbye.

SECOND SHEPHERD   I am so long wakéd, like none in this shire,   260
    I would sleep if I takéd less for my hire.
THIRD SHEPHERD   I am cold and near naked, and would have a fire.

---

228 Fool.
249 Child.

FIRST SHEPHERD   I am weary, for-rakéd,* and run in the mire.
　　Stay awake, you!
SECOND SHEPHERD   Nay, I'll lie down by,　　　　　　　　　265
　　I must sleep must I.
THIRD SHEPHERD   I've as good need to put by
　　As any of you.

　　But, Mak, come hither! Between us must you be.
MAK   You're sure you don't want to talk privately?*　　270
　　Indeed?
　　From my top to my toe,
　　Manus tuas commendo,
　　*Pontio Pilato,**
　　　Christ's cross me speed!　　　　　　　　　　275

　　　　　　(*Then he rises, the shepherds being asleep, and says*)
Now were time for a man that wants for gold
To stealthily enter into a fold,
And nimbly to work then, yet be not too bold,
For he might pay for the bargain, if it were told,　　280
　　At the ending.
Now were time for to spell—
But he needs good counsel
That fain would fare well,
　　And has little spending.　　　　　　　　285

But about you a circle as round as a moon,
Till I've done what I will, till it be noon,
Ye must lie stone still till I have done.
And I shall say thereto of words a few.
　　On height.　　　　　　　　　　　　290
Over your heads my hands I lift:
Your eyes go out and senses drift
Until I make a better shift
　　If it be right.

Lord, how they sleep hard! That may ye all hear.　　295
I never was a shepherd, but now will I learn.
If the flock be scared, when I shall creep near.
How! Draw hitherward! Now mends our cheer
　　From sorrow.
A fat sheep, I dare say;　　　　　　　　　300
A good fleece, dare I lay!

263 Exhausted.
270 Two lines are missing in the ms.
274 "Into thy hands I commend them, Pontius Pilate."

Pay back when I may,
　　But this will I borrow.

(MAK *crosses the stage to his house*)
How, Gill, art thou in? Get us some light.　　　　　　305
WIFE　Who makes such din this time of the night?
I am set for to spin; no hope that I might
Rise a penny to win. I curse them on height.
　　So sore
A housewife thus fares,　　　　　　　　　　　　　310
She always has cares
And all for nothing bears
　　All these chores.

MAK　Good wife, open the latch! Seest thou not what I bring?
WIFE　I'll let thee draw the catch. Ah, come in my sweeting!　315
MAK　Yea, thou dost not reek of my long standing.
WIFE　By thy bare neck for this you're like to swing.
MAK　　　　Go away:
I'm good for something yet,
For in a pinch can I get　　　　　　　　　　　　320
More than they that swink and sweat
　　All the long day.

Thus it fell to my lot, Gill, I had such grace.
WIFE　It were a foul blot to be hanged for the case.
MAK　But I have escaped, Gill, a far narrower place.　　325
WIFE　　Yet so long goes the pot to the water, men say,
　　At last
Comes it home broken.
MAK　Well know I the token,
But let it never be spoken;　　　　　　　　　　　330
　　But come and help fast.

I would he were slain; I want so to eat.
This twelvemonth have I not ta'en of one sheep's meat.
WIFE　Should they come ere he's slain, and hear the sheep bleat—
MAK　Then might I be ta'en! That puts me in a heat!　335
　　Go bar
The gate door.
WIFE　　　　　Yes, Mak,
For if they come at thy back—
MAK　Then might I pay for the pack!　　　　　　　340
May the devil us warn.

WIFE　A good trick have I spied, since thou ken none.
Here shall we him hide tell they be gone—

In my cradle abide. Let me alone,
And I shall lie beside in childbed, and groan. ³⁴⁵
MAK   Thou hast said;
And I'll say thou was light*
Of a male child this night.
WIFE   It's luck I was born bright,
And cleverly bred. ³⁵⁰

For shrewdness this trick can't be surpassed;
Yet a woman's advice always helps at the last!
Before they 'gin to spy, hurry thou fast.
MAK   Unless I come ere they rise, they'll blow a loud blast!
I'll go sleep. ³⁵⁵

      (MAK *returns to the shepherds and resumes his place*)
Yet sleeps all this company;
And I shall go stalk privily,
As it had never been me
    That carried their sheep. ³⁶⁰

FIRST SHEPHERD   *Resurrex a mortuis!** Take hold of my hand.
Judas carnas dominus! I can not well stand;
My foot sleeps, by Jesus; and I'm dry as sand.
I thought we had laid us near English land.
SECOND SHEPHERD   Ah, yea! ³⁶⁵
I slept so well, I feel
As fresh as an eel,
As light on my heel
    As leaf on a tree.

THIRD SHEPHERD   Lord bless us all! My body's all a-quake! ³⁷⁰
My heart jumps from my skin, sure and that's no fake.
Who makes all this din? So my head aches.
I'll teach him something. Hark, fellows, awake!
    We were four.
See ye aught of Mak now? ³⁷⁵
FIRST SHEPHERD   We were up ere thou.
SECOND SHEPHERD   Man, I give God a vow,
    That he went nowhere.

THIRD SHEPHERD   I dreamed he was lapped in a gray wolf's skin.
FIRST SHEPHERD   So many are wrapped now—namely, within. ³⁸⁰
THIRD SHEPHERD   When we had long napped, methought he did begin
A fat sheep to trap; but he made no din.
SECOND SHEPHERD   Be still!

³⁴⁷ Delivered.
³⁶¹ This and the next line are in mock-Latin.

Thy dream makes thee brood;
It's but fancy, by the rood.

FIRST SHEPHERD   Now God turn all to good,
If it be his will! 385

SECOND SHEPHERD   Rise, Mak! For shame! Thou liest right long.
MAK   Now Christ's holy name be us among!
What is this? By Saint James, I may not move along! 390
I think I be the same. Ah! my neck has lain wrong
Enough. (*They help* MAK *up*)
Mickle thanks! Since yestere'en,
Now, by Saint Stephen,
I was flayed with a dream 395
That my heart did cuff.

I thought Gill began to croak and labor full sad,
Indeed at the first cock had borne a young lad
To increase our flock. Guess whether I'm glad;
I am now more in hock than ever I had. 400
Ah, my head!
A house full of bairns!
'Devil knock out their brains!
For father is the pains,
And little bread! 405

I must go home, by your leave, to Gill, as I thought.
I pray you look in my sleeve that I steal naught;
I am loath you to grieve or from you take aught.
THIRD SHEPHERD   Go forth; ill might thou live! Now would I we sought,
This morn, 410
That we had all our store.
FIRST SHEPHERD   But I will go before;
Let us meet.
SECOND SHEPHERD   Where?
THIRD SHEPHERD   At the crooked thorn. 415

(MAK *crosses to his cottage*)
MAK   Undo this door, here! How long shall I stand?
WIFE   Who makes such a stir? Go walk in quicksand!
MAK   Ah, Gill, what cheer? It is I, Mak, your husband.
WIFE   Then may we see here the devil in a band, 420
Sir Guile.
Lo, he comes with a knot
At the back of his crop.*
I'll soon to my cot
For a very long while. 425

[423] An allusion to hanging.

MAK   Will ye hear what she makes to get her a gloze?*
      She does naught but plays, and wiggles her toes.
WIFE Why, who wanders? Who wakes? Who comes? Who goes?
      Who brews? Who bakes? What makes me this hose?
         And then,   430
      It's a pity to behold,
      Now in hot, now in cold,
      Full of woe is the household
         That wants a woman.

      But what end has thou made with the shepherds, Mak?   435
MAK   The last word that they said, when I turned my back,
      They would look that they had their sheep, count the pack.
      I'm sure they'll not be glad to find one they lack,
         Pardie.
      But howsoever it goes,   440
      They will surely suppose,
      From me the trouble 'rose,
         And cry out upon me.
      But thou must do as thou hight.*
WIFE   Of course I will.   445
      I shall swaddle him right; you trust in your Gill.
      If it were a worse plight, yet could I help still.
      I will lie down straight. Come, cover me.
MAK   I will.
WIFE Behind!   450
      It may be a narrow squeak.
MAK   Yes, if too close they peak,
      Or if the sheep should speak!
WIFE   'Tis then time to whine.

      Hearken when they call; for they will come anon.*   455
      Come and make ready all, and sing on thine own;
      Sing lullaby thou shall, for I must groan
      And cry out by the wall on Mary and John,
         For sore.
      Sing a lullaby, fast,   460
      Like thou sang at our last;
      If I play a false cast,
         Trust me no more!

                (*The* SHEPHERDS *meet at the crooked hawthorn*)
THIRD SHEPHERD   Ah, Coll, good morn! Why sleep thou not?   465
FIRST SHEPHERD   Alas, that ever I was born! We have a foul blot.

      426 An excuse.
      444 Promised.
      455 Soon.

A fat lamb have we lorn.*

THIRD SHEPHERD   Marry, God forbid!

SECOND SHEPHERD Who should do us that scorne? That were a foul spot.

FIRST SHEPHERD Some shrew.   470
  I have sought with my dogs
  All Horbury Bogs,
  And with fifteen hogs
    Found I but one ewe.

THIRD SHEPHERD Now trust me if ye will; by Saint Thomas of Kent,   475
  Either Mak or Gill was at that assent.

FIRST SHEPHERD Peace, man, be still! I saw when he went.
  Thou slanders him ill. Thou ought to repent,
    Good speed.

SECOND SHEPHERD Now if ever I lie,   480
  If I should even here die,
  I would say it were he
    That did that same deed.

THIRD SHEPHERD Go we thither, I rede,* at a running trot.
  I shall never eat bread till the truth I've got.   485

FIRST SHEPHERD Nor drink, in my heed, until we solve this plot.

SECOND SHEPHERD Till we know all, indeed, I will rest no jot,
    My brother!
  One thing I will plight:
  Till I see him in sight   490
  Shall I never sleep one night
    Where I do another.

(*At* MAK's *house they hear* GILL *groan and* MAK *sing a lullaby*)

THIRD SHEPHERD Will ye hear how they hack? Our sir likes to croon.

FIRST SHEPHERD Heard I never one crack so clear out of tune!   495
  Call on him.

SECOND SHEPHERD Mak! Undo your door soon.

MAK Who is that spake as it were high noon
    On loft?
  Who is that, I say?   500

THIRD SHEPHERD Good fellows, were it day.

MAK As far as ye may,
    Good, speak soft,

  Over a sick woman's head that is ill at ease;
  I had rather be dead e'er she had any dis-ease.   505

WIFE Go to another place! I may not well wheeze.
  Each foot that ye tread goes to make me sneeze,

467 Lost.
484 Advise.

130 THE WAKEFIELD MASTER

So "he-e-e-e."

FIRST SHEPHERD   Tell us, Mak, if ye may,
How fare ye, I say?   510

MAK   But are ye in town today?
Now how fare ye?

Ye have run in the mire, and are all wet yet.
I shall make you a fire, if ye will sit.
A nurse would I hire, and never doubt it.   515
But at my present hire—well, I hope for a bit
   In season.
I've more bairns than ye knew,
And sure the saying is true,
"We must drink as we brew,"   520
   And that's but reason.

I would ye dined ere ye go. Methinks that ye sweat.

SECOND SHEPHERD   Nay, that mends not our mood, neither drink nor meat.

MAK   Why, what ails you sir?

THIRD SHEPHERD   Yea, our sheep that we get   525
Are stolen as they go. Our loss is not sweet.

MAK   Sirs, drink!
Had I been there,
Someone had paid full dear.

FIRST SHEPHERD   Some men think that ye were;   530
And that makes us think.

SECOND SHEPHERD   Mak, some men say that it should be ye.

THIRD SHEPHERD   Either ye or your spouse; who else could it be?

MAK   Now, if ye suspect us, either Gill or me,
Come and rip our house, and then ye may see   535
   Who had her.
If I any sheep got
Any cow or stott*—
And Gill, my wife, rose not
   Since here she laid her.   540

As I am true and leal,* to God here I pray
That this be the first meal that I shall eat this day.

FIRST SHEPHERD   Mak, as I have weal,* have a care, I say:
"He learned timely to steal that could not say nay."

WIFE   I swelt!*   545
Out, thieves from my home!
Ye come to rob us, ye drones!

---

538 Bullock.   541 Loyal.
543 Riches.
545 Faint.

MAK   Hear ye not how she groans?
      Your heart should melt.

WIFE   Out, thieves, from my bairn! Get out of the door!   550
MAK   Knew ye what she had borne, your hearts would be sore.
      Ye do wrong, I you warn, that thus come before
      To a woman that has borne. But I say no more.
WIFE   Ah, my middle!
      I pray to God so mild,   555
      If ever I you beguiled,
      Let me eat this child
         That lies in this cradle.

MAK   Peace, woman, for God's pain, and cry not so!
      Thou shalt hurt thy brain, and make me full of woe.   560
SECOND SHEPHERD   I think our sheep be slain. Think you not so?
THIRD SHEPHERD   All work we in vain; as well may we go.
      But, drat it,
      I can find no flesh,
      Hard nor nesh,*   565
      Salt nor fresh,
         But two empty platters.

There's no cattle but this, neither tame nor wild,
None, as have I bliss, that smells as he smelled.
WIFE   No, so God me bless, and give me joy of my child!   570
FIRST SHEPHERD   We have marked amiss; I hold us beguiled.
SECOND SHEPHERD   Sir, done.
      Sir, Our Lady him save!
      Is your child a knave?
MAK   Any lord might him crave,   575
      This child as his son.

When he wakens, he skips, that a joy is to see.
THIRD SHEPHERD   In good time be his steps, and happy they be!
      Who were his godfathers, tell now to me?
MAK   So fair fall their lips!   580
FIRST SHEPHERD   Hark now, a lie!
MAK   So God them thank,
      Parkin and Gibbon Waller, I say,
      And gentle John Horn, in good faith,
      He gave all the array   585
         And promised a great shank.

SECOND SHEPHERD   Mak, friends will we be, for we are all one.
MAK   We! Now I hold for me, from you help get I none.

565 Tender.

Farewell, all three! All glad were ye gone! (*The* SHEPHERDS *go out*)

THIRD SHEPHERD   Fair words may there be, but love there is none   590
    This year.
FIRST SHEPHERD   Gave ye the child anything?
SECOND SHEPHERD   I trow,* not one farthing!
THIRD SHEPHERD   Fast back will I fling;
    Abide ye me here.   595

(*The* SHEPHERDS *re-enter the house*)

    Mak, take it to no grief, if I come to thy bairn.
MAK   Nay, thou does me mischief, and foul has thou fared.
THIRD SHEPHERD   The child will not grieve, that little day-star.
    Mak, with your leave, let me give your bairn   600
    But sixpence.
MAK   Nay, go 'way; he sleeps.
THIRD SHEPHERD   Methinks he peeps.
MAK   When he wakens he weeps!
    I pray you, go hence!   605

THIRD SHEPHERD   Give me leave him to kiss, and lift up the clout.*
    What the devil is this? What a monstrous snout!
FIRST SHEPHERD   He is marked amiss. Let's not wait about.
SECOND SHEPHERD   "Ill spun cloth," iwis, "aye comes foul out."
    Aye, so!   610
    He is like to our sheep!
THIRD SHEPHERD   How, Gib, may I peep?
FIRST SHEPHERD   I trow, nature will creep
    Where it may not go!

SECOND SHEPHERD   This was a quaint fraud, and a far cast!   615
    It should be noised abroad.
THIRD SHEPHERD   Yea, sirs, and classed.
    Let's burn this bawd, and bind her fast.
    Everyone will applaud to hang her at last,
    So shall thou.   620
    Will ye see how they swaddle
    His four feet in the middle?
    Saw I never in cradle
    A horned lad ere now.

MAK   Peace, peace, I ask. You'll give the child a scare.   625
    For I am his father, and yon woman him bare.
FIRST SHEPHERD   After what devil shall he be called? "Mak?" Lo, Mak's heir!
SECOND SHEPHERD   Let be all that. Now God give him care,
    I say.

593 Assert as true: admit.
606 Cloth.

WIFE A pretty child is he   630
 To sit on a woman's knee;
 A dilly-downe, pardie,
  To make a father gay.

THIRD SHEPHERD I know him by the ear-mark; that's a good token.
MAK I tell you, sirs, hark! His nose was broken;   635
 Later told me a clerk that he was forespoken.*
FIRST SHEPHERD Liar! You deserve to have your noddle broken!
 Get a weapon.
WIFE He was taken by an elf,
 I saw it myself;   640
 When the clock struck twelve
  He was misshapen.

SECOND SHEPHERD Ye two are well made to lie in the same bed.
THIRD SHEPHERD Since they maintain their theft, let's see them both dead.
MAK If I do wrong again, cut off my head!   645
 I'm at your will.
FIRST SHEPHERD   Sirs, take this plan, instead,
 For this trespass:
 We'll neither curse nor fight,
 Quarrel nor chide,   650
 But seize him tight
  And cast him in canvas.
   (*They toss* MAK *in a sheet and go back to the fields*)

FIRST SHEPHERD Lord, but I am sore; I feel about to burst.
 In faith, I may no more; therefore will I rest.   655
SECOND SHEPHERD As a sheep of seven score he weighed in my fist.
 Now to sleep anywhere methinks were the best.
THIRD SHEPHERD Now I pray you,
 Let's lie down on this green.
FIRST SHEPHERD Oh, these thieves are so keen.   660
THIRD SHEPHERD Let's forget what has been,
 So I say you. (*They sleep*)

  (*An* ANGEL *sings "Gloria in excelsis"; then let him say*)
ANGEL Rise, herd-men kind! For now is he born
 That shall take from the fiend what Adam had lorn: 665
 That devil to shame this night is he born;
 God is made your friend now at this morn.
  He behests
 To Bethlehem go ye,
 Where lies the Free;*   670

---

⁶³⁶ Bewitched.
⁶⁷⁰ The Divine One.

134 THE WAKEFIELD MASTER

In a manger he'll be
     Between two beasts.

FIRST SHEPHERD   This was a sweet voice as any I've heard.
     A wonder enough to make a man scared.
SECOND SHEPHERD   To speak of God's son from on high he dared.   675
     All the wood on the moor with lightning glared,
          Everywhere.
THIRD SHEPHERD   He said the babe lay
     In Bethlehem today.
FIRST SHEPHERD   That star points the way.   680
     Let us seek him there.

SECOND SHEPHERD   Say, what was his song? Heard ye not how he cracked it,
     Three briefs to a long?*
THIRD SHEPHERD   Yea, marry, he hacked it;
     Was no crotchet* wrong, nor nothing that lacked it.   685
FIRST SHEPHERD   For to sing us among, right as he knacked it*
     I can.
SECOND SHEPHERD   Let's see how ye croon.
     Can ye bark at the moon?
THIRD SHEPHERD   Hold your tongues, have done!   690
FIRST SHEPHERD   Hark after, then!

SECOND SHEPHERD   To Bethlehem he bade that we should go;
     I am full afeared that we have been too slow.
THIRD SHEPHERD   Be merry and not sad; for sure this we know,
     This news means joy to us men below,   695
          Of no joy.
FIRST SHEPHERD   Therefore thither hie we,
     Be we wet and weary,
     To that child and that lady.
          We must see this boy.   700

SECOND SHEPHERD   We find by the prophecy—let be your din!
     Of David and Isaiah and others of their kin,
     They prophesied by clergy that in a virgin
     Should he light and lie, to slacken our sin
          And slake it,   705
     Our Race from woe.
     For Isaiah said so:
     "Ecce virgo
          *Concipiet"** a child that is naked.

---

683 Musical notes.
685 A quarter note.
686 Did it cleverly.
709 "Behold, a virgin shall conceive." Cf. *Isaiah,* 7, 14; *St. Luke,* 1, 31; and *St. Matthew,* 1, 23.

THIRD SHEPHERD   Full glad may we be that this is that day   710
   Him lovely to see, who rules for aye.
   Lord, happy I'd be if I could say
   That I knelt on my knee so that I might pray
     To that child.
   But the angel said,   715
   He was poorly arrayed,
   And in a manger laid,
     Both humble and mild.

FIRST SHEPHERD   Patriarchs and prophets of old were torn
   With yearning to see this child that is born.   720
   They are gone full clean, and their trouble they've lorn.
   But we shall see him, I ween,* ere it be morn,
     To token.
   When I see him and feel,
   Then know I full well   725
   It is true as steel
     That prophets have spoken:

   To so poor as we are that he would appear,
   To find us and tell us by his messenger!
SECOND SHEPHERD   Go we now, let us fare, for the place is near.   730
THIRD SHEPHERD   I am ready, prepared; let us go with good cheer
     To that bright
   Lord, if thy will be—
   We are simple all three—
   Grant us some kind of glee   735
     To comfort thy wight.* (*They enter the stable*)

FIRST SHEPHERD   Hail, comely and clean! Hail, young child!
   Hail, Maker, as I mean, born of maiden so mild!
   Thou has cursed, I ween, the devil so wild;
   The false guiler of men, now goes he beguiled.   740
     Lo, he merry is!
   Look, he laughs, the sweeting!
   Well, to this meeting
   I bring as my greeting
     A bob of cherries!   745

SECOND SHEPHERD   Hail, sovereign Savior, our ransom thou hast bought!
   Hail, noble child and flower, that all things has wrought!
   Hail, full of favor, that made all of naught!
   Hail! I kneel and I cower. A bird have I brought
     To my bairn.   750

---

722 I imagine.
736 Man.

Hail, little tiny mop!
Of our creed thou art crop.
I would drink of thy cup,
     Little day-star.

THIRD SHEPHERD   Hail, darling dear, thou art God indeed!   755
     I pray thee be near when that I have need.
     Hail! Sweet is thy cheer! My heart would bleed
     To see thee lie here in so poor a weed,
          With no pennies.
     I would give thee my all,   760
     Though I bring but a ball;
     Have and play thee withal,
          And go to the tennis.

MARY   The Father of Heaven, God omnipotent,
     That set all in seven days, his Son has sent.   765
     My name he has blessed with peace ere he went.
     I conceived him through grace as God had meant;
          And now he's born.
     I shall pray him so
     To keep you all from woe!   770
     Tell this wherever ye go,
          And mind this morn.

FIRST SHEPHERD   Farewell, lady, so fair to behold,
     With thy child on thy knee!
SECOND SHEPHERD   Still he lies full cold.   775
     Lord, how favored I be. Now we go forth, behold.
THIRD SHEPHERD   Forsooth, already this seems a thing told
     Full oft.
FIRST SHEPHERD   What grace we have found!
SECOND SHEPHERD   Spread the tidings around!   780
THIRD SHEPHERD   To sing are we bound:
     Let take aloft! (*They sing*)

Andrieu de la Vigne

Andrieu de la Vigne (c.1450–c.1515) *was a courtier and aide to King Charles VIII, as well as a dabbler in letters. His work in farce in* THE BLIND MAN AND THE CRIPPLE *exemplifies the excellence of production in that form during the late fifteenth and sixteenth centuries in France. During this period hundreds, perhaps more, of these short, lively plays were written and performed, usually by amateur Companies of Fools or small professional troupes. The best of them rank with the best farces anywhere for liveliness of invention and exuberance of comic spirit. In addition to this play, Andrieu wrote a mystery play, poems, and a curious, allegorical travel book.*

Chronology

*c.*1450 Born at La Rochelle.

1475–90 Served as secretary to the Duke of Savoy and later to Anne of Brittany; then named Orator of the King to Charles VIII.

1493 Accompanied King Charles on his expedition to Naples. At the king's order he kept a journal of the trip which was later published as part of his miscellany-allegory-travel-book-history entitled *The Garden of Honor.*

1496 Wrote *The Miracle of the Blind Man and the Cripple* and a *Mystery of St. Martin,* which were produced at Seurre.

*c.*1508 Probable year of his *Ballades Concerning Rumors about the Alliances of Kings.*

1513 Published the *Epitaphs in Rondeau Form on the Death of the Queen.*

*c.*1515 Probable year of his death.

THE MIRACLE OF
THE BLIND MAN
AND
THE CRIPPLE

by Andrieu de la Vigne

Translated by Henry W. Wells and Roger S. Loomis

Characters
BLIND MAN
CRIPPLE
Clerics
Crowd

BLIND MAN   Alms for one penniless and blind,
  Who never yet hath seen at all!
CRIPPLE   Pray, to the poor lame man be kind!
  With gout he cannot trudge or crawl.
BLIND MAN   Alas, right here I'll fade away   5
  Without a varlet to attend me.
CRIPPLE   I cannot budge, ah, welladay!
  Good God, preserve Thou and defend me.
BLIND MAN   That rascal who led me astray
  And left me here all empty-handed,   10
  He was a goodly guide, ifay!*
  To rob me and then leave me stranded.
CRIPPLE   Alack, I'm in a pretty scrape!
  How shall I win my livelihood?
  I cannot from this spot escape,   15
  However much I wish I could.
BLIND MAN   Meseems I here shall fast all day.
  Unless I find a varlet faster.
CRIPPLE   Bad Luck has picked me for her prey,
  And now she has become my master.   20
BLIND MAN   For this desirable situation
  Can't I get even one application?
  I've had one varlet in my day
  I trusted. He was called Giblet.

¹¹ In faith.

Jolly he was and on the level,
Though ugly as the very devil.
I lost a treasure when he left me.
Plague on the plague that thus bereft me.
CRIPPLE   Will no one help me in my need?
For God's love, pity my estate.
BLIND MAN   Who are you that so loudly plead?
Good friend, betake you hither straight.
CRIPPLE   Alas, I'm planted in this spot,
Right in the middle of the street,
And cannot move. Saint Matthew, what
A wretched life!
BLIND MAN   Come stir your feet
Along this way: 'twill bring you luck.
Let's see what mirth we can discover.
CRIPPLE   Your tongue wags easily, my chuck.
But mirth and joy for us are over.
BLIND MAN   Come hither; we shall make great cheer,
An't please the Lord of Paradise.
And though like blunderers we appear,
We'll harm no man in any wise.
CRIPPLE   My friend, you throw your words away.
For hence I cannot budge an inch.
God curse them on the judgment day
By whom I got into this pinch.
BLIND MAN   If I could walk in your direction
I'd gladly carry you a bit—
(At least, if I had strength for it)—
To give you easement and protection.
And you could succor me in turn
By guiding me from place to place.
CRIPPLE   This is no plan to lightly spurn.
You've said the best thing for our case.
BLIND MAN   I'll walk straight towards you if I can.
Is this the right way?
CRIPPLE   Yes, don't stumble.
BLIND MAN   Methinks it is a better plan
To go on all fours and not tumble.
I'm headed right?
CRIPPLE   Straight as a quail.
You'll soon be here in front of me.
BLIND MAN   When I come near you, do not fail
To give your hand.
CRIPPLE   I will, pardie.*
Stop, you're not going straight, turn hither.
BLIND MAN   This way?

[68] By God; indeed.

CRIPPLE   No, No! Turn to the right.

BLIND MAN   So?

CRIPPLE   Yes.

BLIND MAN   It puts me in high feather,
Good sir, at last to hold you tight.   75
Now will you mount upon my back?
I trow* well I can bear the pack.

CRIPPLE   So much I must in you confide;
Then I in turn can be your guide.

BLIND MAN   Are you well set?   80

CRIPPLE   By Mary, yes.
Look well you do not let me fall.

BLIND MAN   If I should show such carelessness,
Pray God may evil me befall.
But guide aright.   85

CRIPPLE   Yes, by my troth.
Look, here's my staff with iron shod.
Take it. And here I give my oath
To guide you faithfully, by God.

BLIND MAN   Lord, had I known how much you weighed!   90
Wherefore is this?

CRIPPLE   Plod on, good fellow
And keep the bargain that we made.
D'you hear? Get up!

BLIND MAN   That's all quite well—Oh   95
But what a load!

CRIPPLE   But what a lie!
A feather's not more light than I.

BLIND MAN   Hold on, by God's blood; get a clutch,
Or else I'll drop you! Never yet   100
Did blacksmith's anvil weigh so much.
Get down; I'm in an awful sweat. . . . (CRIPPLE *reluctantly gets down*)
Hey, what's the news?

CRIPPLE   What did you say?
They tell a really sumptuous thing.   105
A saint has lately passed away,
Whose works are most astonishing.
He heals the gravest maladies
Of which you ever yet heard speak—
That's if the sick are good and meek.   110
I here defy these powers of his.

BLIND MAN   What's that you're telling?

CRIPPLE   What's the joke?
It's said if the corpse comes this way
I should be cured all at one stroke,   115
And you too, likewise. Now I pray,

⁷⁷ Believe.

Come hither. If 'twere really so
That we were healed of all our woe,
Far harder then 'twould be to gain
Our livelihood than now.   120

BLIND MAN   Nay, nay.
That he may heal us of our pain
Let us go where he is, I say,
And find the corpse.

CRIPPLE   Were I assured   125
That we should not be healed by him,
Right well I'd go. But to be cured
And strong, I will not stir a limb.
No, we had better find our way
Out of this place.   130

BLIND MAN   What's this about?

CRIPPLE   Why, when I'm cured, I'll waste away
Of hunger. Everyone will shout:
"Be off, and do some honest labor."
No, you'll not find me that saint's neighbor!   135
For if he fixed me up, they'll call
Me vagabond, and one would bawl:
"That brazen rascal, sound of limb,
The galleys are the place for him."

BLIND MAN   So glib a tongue I never saw.   140
Yet I confess it speaks good sense.
You have the gift of eloquence.

CRIPPLE   I tell you, I care not a straw
To go and have the corpse remove
My malady.   145

BLIND MAN   Yea, 'twould be folly
To seek it, and we will not move.

CRIPPLE   I dare pledge, if it cured you wholly,
In a short time you'd feel regret.
Folk would not give you anything   150
But bread, and never would you get
A tasty bit.

BLIND MAN   May heaven bring
Some great doom on my head, or let
Them strip from off my skin   155
Enough for two belts ere I'd set
My eyes on it!

CRIPPLE   Think, too, how thin
Your purse would be.

BLIND MAN   Yea, that I trow.   160

CRIPPLE   Never a day but we'd be pining
And there'd be not a penny to show.

BLIND MAN   Yea, truly?

CRIPPLE   By the Cross, I swear
    It will be even as I'm divining.   165
BLIND MAN   Since you have counseled me so fair,
    Henceforth your word I'll never doubt.
CRIPPLE   The body's in the church they say:
    We must not venture thereabout.
BLIND MAN   If ever we are caught in there   170
    May Satan carry us away!

                          (*Pause*)

CRIPPLE   Come, down this alley let us toddle.
BLIND MAN   Whither?
CRIPPLE   This way.   175
BLIND MAN   Let us not wait.
CRIPPLE   My faith, 'twould show an empty noddle
    To seek the saint out in his lair.
BLIND MAN   Let us be off.
CRIPPLE   Which way?   180
BLIND MAN   Why straight
    Where this old toper winters merrily.
CRIPPLE   A wise word have you spoken verily.
    Where go we?
BLIND MAN   To the tavern. There   185
    Without a lantern I can totter.
CRIPPLE   I tell you, even so can I.
    Give me an ale-house when I'm dry
    Before a cistern full of water.
BLIND MAN   Listen, I say!   190
CRIPPLE   Listen to what?
BLIND MAN   Whatever's making that todo?
CRIPPLE   If it's the body!
BLIND MAN   Horrible thought!
    No longer we'd be catered to.   195
    Hark!
CRIPPLE   After it the whole town chases.
BLIND MAN   Go look what's making all the pother.
CRIPPLE   Bad luck is close upon our traces.
    Good master, it's the saint, no other!   200
BLIND MAN   Quick, let's be off: we must not bide.
    I fear he'll catch us after all.
CRIPPLE   Under some window let us hide,
    Or in the corner of a wall.
    Look out, don't trip!   205
BLIND MAN (*Falling down*) The devil's in it!
    To fall at such an awkward minute!
CRIPPLE   Pray God he do not find us here:
    Too cruel then would be our state.
BLIND MAN   My heart is bitten through with fear.   210

We've fallen upon an evil fate.
CRIPPLE   Lie low, my master, take good care,
And we'll crawl off beneath some stair.
(*Procession of clergy, bearing body of saint in a reliquary, passes, followed by crowd. Exeunt*)   215
BLIND MAN (*Looking at the reliquary*):
I'm henceforth in this good saint's debt.
I see as never I saw before.
What a great fool I was to let
Myself be cozened into fleeing.   220
There's nothing, search the wide world o'er,
That to my mind's as good as seeing.
CRIPPLE   The Devil take him in his chain!
He knows no gratitude nor grace.
Better if I had spared the pain   225
Of coming to this cursed place.
Alas, I'm quite at my wit's end.
Hunger will put me in my grave.
With rage I claw my face and rend.
Damnation on the whoreson knave!   230
BLIND MAN   I was a very dunderhead
To leave the good safe road and tread
The doubtful bypath, wandering.
Alas, full little had I guessed
That clear sight was so great a thing.   235
Now I can look on fair Savoy
And Burgundy and France the blest.
Humbly I thank God for this joy.
CRIPPLE   What an unlucky turn for me!
I never yet to work was taught.   240
This day has turned out wretchedly,
And I'm a wretch to be so caught.
So I am caught in Fortune's trap,
Not wise enough to dodge its snap.
Unfortunately I'm too wise   245
On my bad luck to shut my eyes.
BLIND MAN   The rumor of thy power to bless,
St. Martin, has been spread so wide
That folk crowd in from every side,
This morning, toward thy holiness.   250
I thank thee not in Latin tongue
But in live French—thou art so kind.
If to thy mercy I've been blind,
Pardon I beg for this great wrong.
CRIPPLE   Well, here I have a sweet new figure.   255
But you'll not have so long to wait
Before I'll manage to disfigure

This pretty form of mine once more.
I've stored up in this little pate
The use of herbs, and all the learning   260
I need to raise with oils a sore
Upon my leg, such that you'll vow
That with Saint Anthony's fire* it's burning.
I'll make myself more sleek than lard,—
Don't think that I don't know the way,—   265
And there'll not be a man so hard
But will be melted with compassion.
Then too, I'm expert in the role
Of one whose body's one huge ache.
"In honor of the Sacred Passion,"   270
I'll quaver, "look at this poor soul,
And see these tortured members shake."
Then I'll tell how I've been at Rome,
How the Turks locked me up at Acre,
And how I'm here so far from home   275
On pilgrimage to St. Fiacre.*

---

[263] Any of several inflammations or gangrenous conditions of the skin; so called because it was believed that St. Anthony had special powers to cure them.

[276] A shrine to the saint at the Cathedral of Meaux, near Paris. St. Fiacre was also reputed to have healing powers.

The Morality Play

Everyman (*c.1475*) *is the supreme example in English of the medieval morality play. Perhaps derived from an earlier Dutch play, or perhaps from a long line of such plays, the play owes its allegorical form to the widespread popularity of this mode in the Middle Ages, as well as, perhaps, to such earlier dramatic forms as the Paternoster play. Nothing is known of its author, but it is assumed to have been written by a cleric or clerics, who in the early years of the morality play's popularity used the form as yet another way of teaching Catholic doctrine.*

Selected Bibliography

Kaula, David, "Time and the Timeless in *Everyman* and *Dr. Faustus*," *College English*, XXII (1959), 9–14.

Ryan, Lawrence V., "Doctrine and Dramatic Structure in *Everyman*," *Speculum*, XXXII (1957), 722–735.

Van Laan, Thomas F., "*Everyman*: A Structural Analysis," *PMLA*, LXXVIII (1962), 465–475.

EVERYMAN

Anonymous

Characters
MESSENGER
GOD: ADONAI
DEATH
EVERYMAN
FELLOWSHIP
COUSIN
KINDRED
GOODS
GOOD DEEDS
KNOWLEDGE
CONFESSION
BEAUTY
STRENGTH
DISCRETION
FIVE WITS
ANGEL
DOCTOR

Here beginneth a treatise how the High Father of Heaven sendeth Death to summon every creature to come and give account of their lives in this world, and is in manner of a moral play.

(*Enter* MESSENGER *as Prologue*)

MESSENGER   I pray you all give your audience,
And hear this matter with reverence,
By figure a moral play—
The *Summoning of Everyman* called it is,
That of our lives and ending shows   5
How transitory we be all day.
This matter is wondrous precious,
But the intent of it is more gracious,
And sweet to bear away.
The story saith:—Man, in the beginning,   10
Look well, and take good heed to the ending,
Be you never so gay!
Ye think sin in the beginning full sweet,
Which in the end causeth thy soul to weep,
When the body lieth in clay.   15
Here shall you see how Fellowship and Jollity,

Both Strength, Pleasure, and Beauty,
Will fade from thee as flower in May.
For ye shall hear how our Heaven King
Calleth Everyman to a general reckoning. 20
Give audience, and hear what he doth say. (*Exit*)
(GOD *speaks from above*)

GOD   I perceive, here in my majesty,
How that all creatures be to me unkind,
Living without dread in worldly prosperity; 25
Of ghostly sight the people be so blind,
Drowned in sin, they know me not for their God.
In worldly riches is all their mind,
They fear not my righteousness, the sharp rod;
My love that I showed when I for them died 30
They forget clean, and shedding of my blood red;
I hanged between two, it cannot be denied;
To get them life I suffered to be dead;
I healed their feet, with thorns hurt was my head.
I could do no more than I did, truly; 35
And now I see the people do clean forsake me.
They use the seven deadly sins damnable;
As pride, covetise, wrath, and lechery,
Now in the world be made commendable;
And thus they leave of angels, the heavenly company. 40
Everyman liveth so after his own pleasure,
And yet of their life they be nothing sure.
I see the more that I them forbear
The worse they be from year to year;
All that liveth appaireth* fast. 45
Therefore I will, in all the haste,
Have a reckoning of Everyman's person;
For, and I leave the people thus alone
In their life and wicked tempests,
Verily they will become much worse than beasts; 50
For now one would by envy another up eat;
Charity they all do clean forget.
I hoped well that Everyman
In my glory should make his mansion,
And thereto I had them all elect; 55
But now I see, like traitors deject,
They thank me not for the pleasure that I to them meant,
Nor yet for their being that I them have lent.
I proffered the people great multitude of mercy,
And few there be that asketh it heartily; 60
They be so cumbered with worldly riches,

45 Becomes impaired.

That needs on them I must do justice,
On everyman living, without fear.
Where art thou, Death, thou mighty messenger?

(*Enter* DEATH)

65

DEATH Almighty God, I am here at your will,
Your commandment to fulfil.

GOD Go thou to Everyman,
And show him, in my name,
A pilgrimage he must on him take,
Which he in no wise may escape;
And that he bring with him a sure reckoning
Without delay or any tarrying.

DEATH Lord, I will in the world go run over all,
And cruelly out search both great and small. (GOD *withdraws*)
Every man will I beset that liveth beastly
Out of God's laws, and dreadeth not folly.
He that loveth riches I will strike with my dart,
His sight to blind, and from heaven to depart,
Except that alms be his good friend,
In hell for to dwell, world without end.

(*Enter* EVERYMAN, *at a distance*)

Lo, yonder I see Everyman walking;
Full little he thinketh on my coming;
His mind is on fleshly lusts and his treasure;
And great pain it shall cause him to endure
Before the Lord, Heaven King.
Everyman, stand still; whither art thou going
Thus gaily? Hast thou thy Maker forgot?

EVERYMAN Why askest thou?
Wouldest thou wete?*

DEATH Yea, sir, I will show you;
In great haste I am sent to thee
From God out of his Majesty.

EVERYMAN What, sent to me?

DEATH Yea, certainly.
Though thou have forgot him here,
He thinketh on thee in the heavenly sphere,
As, or we depart, thou shalt know.

EVERYMAN What desireth God of me?

DEATH That shall I show thee;
A reckoning he will needs have
Without any longer respite.

EVERYMAN To give a reckoning longer leisure I crave;
This blind* matter troubleth my wit.

⁹¹ Know.
¹⁰⁵ Obscure.

DEATH　On thee thou must take a long journey,
　　Therefore thy book of count* with thee thou bring;
　　For turn again thou can not by no way.
　　And look thou be sure of thy reckoning;
　　For before God thou shalt answer and show　　　　　　　　110
　　Thy many bad deeds, and good but a few,
　　How thou hast spent thy life, and in what wise,
　　Before the Chief Lord of paradise.
　　Have ado that we were in that way,
　　For, wete thou well, thou shalt make none attournay.*　　115
EVERYMAN　Full unready I am such reckoning to give.
　　I know thee not. What messenger art thou?
DEATH　I am Death, that no man dreadeth.*
　　For every man I rest,* and no man spareth;
　　For it is God's commandment　　　　　　　　　　　120
　　That all to me should be obedient.
EVERYMAN　O Death! thou comest when I had thee least in mind;
　　In thy power it lieth me to save,
　　Yet of my goods will I give thee, if thou will be kind;
　　Yea, a thousand pound shalt thou have,　　　　　　　125
　　And defer this matter till another day.
DEATH　Everyman, it may not be, by no way;
　　I set not by gold, silver, nor riches,
　　Nor by pope, emperor, king, duke, nor princes.
　　For, and I would receive gifts great,　　　　　　　　130
　　All the world I might get;
　　But my custom is clean contrary.
　　I give thee no respite. Come hence, and not tarry.
EVERYMAN　Alas! shall I have no longer respite?
　　I may say Death giveth no warning.　　　　　　　　135
　　To think on thee, it maketh my heart sick,
　　For all unready is my book of reckoning.
　　But twelve year and I might have abiding,
　　My counting-book I would make so clear,
　　That my reckoning I should not need to fear.　　　　　140
　　Wherefore, Death, I pray thee, for God's mercy,
　　Spare me till I be provided of remedy.
DEATH　Thee availeth not to cry, weep, and pray;
　　But haste thee lightly that you were gone that journey,
　　And prove thy friends if thou can.　　　　　　　　145
　　For wete thou well the tide abideth no man;
　　And in the world each living creature
　　For Adam's sin must die of nature.

[107] Account book.
[115] That is, "You shall not play the lawyer."
[118] Who respects no man.
[119] Arrest.

150　ANONYMOUS

EVERYMAN   Death, if I should this pilgrimage take,
   And my reckoning surely make,   150
   Show me, for Saint Charity,
   Should I not come again shortly?
DEATH   No, Everyman; and thou be once there,
   Thou mayst never more come here,
   Trust me verily.   155
EVERYMAN   O gracious God, in the high seat celestial,
   Have mercy on me in this most need;
   Shall I have no company from this vale terrestrial
   Of mine acquaintance that way me to lead?
DEATH   Yea, if any be so hardy,   160
   That would go with thee and bear thee company.
   Hie thee that thou were gone to God's magnificence,
   Thy reckoning to give before his presence.
   What! weenest* thou thy life is given thee,
   And thy worldy goods also?   165
EVERYMAN   I had weened so, verily.
DEATH   Nay, nay; it was but lent thee;
   For, as soon as thou art gone,
   Another a while shall have it, and then go therefrom
   Even as thou hast done.   170
   Everyman, thou art mad! thou hast thy wits five,
   And here on earth will not amend thy life;
   For suddenly I do come.
EVERYMAN   O wretched caitiff! whither shall I flee,
   That I might 'scape this endless sorrow!   175
   Now, gentle Death, spare me till tomorrow,
   That I may amend me
   With good advisement.
DEATH   Nay; thereto I will not consent,
   Nor no man will I respite,   180
   But to the heart suddenly I shall smite
   Without any advisement.
   And now out of thy sight I will me hie;
   See thou make thee ready shortly,
   For thou mayst say this is the day   185
   That no man living may 'scape away. (*Exit* DEATH)
EVERYMAN   Alas! I may well weep with sighs deep;
   Now have I no manner of company
   To help me in my journey and me to keep;
   And also my writing is full unready.   190
   How shall I do now for to excuse me?
   I would to God I had never been gete!*
   To my soul a full great profit it had be;

164 Do you suppose.
192 Been begotten; born.

For now I fear pains huge and great.
The time passeth; Lord, help, that all wrought;   195
For though I mourn it availeth naught.
The day passeth, and is almost a-go;
I wot not well what for to do.
To whom were I best my complaint to make?
What and I to Fellowship thereof spake,   200
And showed him of this sudden chance?
For in him is all mine affiance;*
We have in the world so many a day
Been good friends in sport and play.
I see him yonder, certainly;   205
I trust that he will bear me company;
Therefore to him will I speak to ease my sorrow.

(Enter FELLOWSHIP)

Well met, good Fellowship, and good morrow!

FELLOWSHIP   Everyman, good morrow; by this day!   210
Sir, why lookest thou so piteously?
If any thing be amiss, I pray thee me say,
That I may help to remedy.

EVERYMAN   Yea, good Fellowship, yea,
I am in great jeopardy.   215

FELLOWSHIP   My true friend, show to me your mind;
I will not forsake thee, unto my life's end,
In the way of good company.

EVERYMAN   That was well spoken, and lovingly.

FELLOWSHIP   Sir, I must needs know your heaviness;   220
I have pity to see you in any distress;
If any have you wronged, ye shall revenged be,
Though I on the ground be slain for thee,
Though that I know before that I should die.

EVERYMAN   Verily, Fellowship, gramercy.*   225

FELLOWSHIP   Tush! by thy thanks I set not a straw!
Show me your grief, and say no more.

EVERYMAN   If I my heart should to you break,
And then you to turn your mind from me,
And would not me comfort when you hear me speak,   230
Then should I ten times sorrier be.

FELLOWSHIP   Sir, I say as I will do, indeed.

EVERYMAN   Then be you a good friend at need;
I have found you true here before.

FELLOWSHIP   And so ye shall evermore;   235
For, in faith, and thou go to hell
I will not forsake thee by the way!

EVERYMAN   Ye speak like a good friend; I believe you well;

---

202 Trust.
225 Many thanks.

I shall deserve it, and I may.

FELLOWSHIP   I speak of no deserving, by this day.   240
For he that will say and nothing do
Is not worthy with good company to go;
Therefore show me the grief of your mind,
As to your friend most loving and kind.

EVERYMAN   I shall show you how it is;   245
Commanded I am to go a journey,
A long way, hard and dangerous,
And give a strait count without delay
Before the high judge, Adonai.*
Wherefore, I pray you, bear me company,   250
As ye have promised, in this journey.

FELLOWSHIP   That is matter indeed! Promise is duty;
But, and I should take such a voyage on me,
I know it well, it should be to my pain.
Also it maketh me afeared, certain.   255
But let us take counsel here as well as we can,
For your words would fear a strong man.

EVERYMAN   Why, ye said if I had need,
Ye would me never forsake, quick nor dead,
Though it were to hell, truly.   260

FELLOWSHIP   So I said, certainly,
But such pleasures be set aside, the sooth to say.
And also, if we took such a journey,
When should we come again?

EVERYMAN   Nay, never again till the day of doom.   265

FELLOWSHIP   In faith, then will not I come there!
Who hath you these tidings brought?

EVERYMAN   Indeed, Death was with me here.

FELLOWSHIP   Now, by God that all hath bought,
If Death were the messenger,   270
For no man that is living today
I will not go that loath journey—
Not for the father that begat me!

EVERYMAN   Ye promised otherwise, pardie.

FELLOWSHIP   I wot well I said so, truly;   275
And yet if thou wilt eat, and drink, and make good cheer,
Or haunt to women the lusty company,
I would not forsake you while the day is clear,
Trust me verily!

EVERYMAN   Yea, thereto ye would be ready;   280
To go to mirth, solace, and play,
Your mind will sooner apply
Than to bear me company in my long journey.

FELLOWSHIP   Now, in good faith, I will not that way.

---

249 Hebrew name for God in the *Old Testament*.

But and thou wilt murder, or any man kill, 285
In that I will help thee with a good will!
EVERYMAN   O, that is a simple advice indeed!
Gentle Fellow, help me in my necessity;
We have loved long, and now I need,
And now, gentle Fellowship, remember me! 290
FELLOWSHIP   Whether ye have loved me or no,
By Saint John, I will not with thee go.
EVERYMAN   Yet, I pray thee, take the labor, and do so much for me
To bring me forward, for Saint Charity,
And comfort me till I come without the town. 295
FELLOWSHIP   Nay, and thou would give me a new gown,
I will not a foot with thee go;
But, and thou had tarried, I would not have left thee so.
And as now God speed thee in thy journey,
For from thee I will depart as fast as I may. 300
EVERYMAN   Whither away, Fellowship? Will you forsake me?
FELLOWSHIP   Yea, by my fay,* to God I betake thee.
EVERYMAN   Farewell, good Fellowship; for thee my heart is sore;
Adieu for ever! I shall see thee no more.
FELLOWSHIP   In faith, Everyman, farewell now at the end; 305
For you I will remember that parting is mourning. (*Exit* FELLOWSHIP)
EVERYMAN   Alack! shall we thus depart indeed?
(Ah, Lady, help!) without any more comfort,
Lo, Fellowship forsaketh me in my most need.
For help in this world whither shall I resort? 310
Fellowship herebefore with me would merry make,
And now little sorrow for me doth he take.
It is said, "In prosperity men friends may find,
Which in adversity be full unkind."
Now whither for succor shall I flee, 315
Sith* that Fellowship hath forsaken me?
To my kinsmen I will, truly,
Praying them to help me in my necessity;
I believe that they will do so,
For "kind will creep where it may not go." 320
I will go say, for yonder I see them go.
Where be ye now, my friends and kinsmen?
                    (*Enter* KINDRED *and* COUSIN)
KINDRED   Here be we now, at your commandment.
Cousin, I pray you show us your intent 325
In any wise, and do not spare.
COUSIN   Yea, Everyman, and to us declare
If ye be disposed to go any whither,
For, wete you well, we will live and die together.

302 Faith.
316 Since.

KINDRED   In wealth and woe we will with you hold,   330
     For over his kin a man may be bold.
EVERYMAN   Gramercy, my friends and kinsmen kind.
     Now shall I show you the grief of my mind.
     I was commanded by a messenger
     That is an high king's chief officer;   335
     He bade me go a pilgrimage, to my pain,
     And I know well I shall never come again;
     Also I must give a reckoning straight,
     For I have a great enemy that hath me in wait,
     Which intendeth me for to hinder.   340
KINDRED   What account is that which ye must render?
     That would I know.
EVERYMAN   Of all my works I must show
     How I have lived, and my days spent;
     Also of ill deeds that I have used   345
     In my time, sith life was me lent;
     And of all virtues that I have refused.
     Therefore I pray you go thither with me,
     To help to make mine account, for Saint Charity.
COUSIN   What, to go thither? Is that the matter?   350
     Nay, Everyman, I had liefer* fast bread and water
     All this five year and more.
EVERYMAN   Alas, that ever I was bore!
     For now shall I never be merry
     If that you forsake me.   355
KINDRED   Ah, sir; what, ye be a merry man!
     Take good heart to you, and make no moan.
     But one thing I warn you, by Saint Anne,
     As for me, ye shall go alone.
EVERYMAN   My Cousin, will you not with me go?   360
COUSIN   No, by our Lady; I have the cramp in my toe.
     Trust not to me; for, so God me speed,
     I will deceive you in your most need.
KINDRED   It availeth not us to tice.*
     Ye shall have my maid with all my heart;   365
     She loveth to go to feasts, there to be nice,
     And to dance, and abroad to start;
     I will give her leave to help you in that journey,
     If that you and she may agree.
EVERYMAN   Now show me the very effect of your mind.   370
     Will you go with me, or abide behind?
KINDRED   Abide behind? yea, that will I, and I may!
     Therefore farewell till another day. (*Exit* KINDRED)
EVERYMAN   How should I be merry or glad?

351 Rather.
364 Entice.

For fair promises men to me make,   375
But when I have most need, they me forsake.
I am deceived; that maketh me sad.

COUSIN   Cousin Everyman, farewell now,
For verily I will not go with you;
Also of mine own life an unready reckoning   380
I have to account; therefore I make tarrying.
Now, God keep thee, for now I go. (*Exit* COUSIN)

EVERYMAN   Ah, Jesus! is all come hereto?
Lo, fair words maketh fools fain;*
They promise and nothing will do certain.   385
My kinsmen promised me faithfully
For to abide with me steadfastly,
And now fast away do they flee:
Even so Fellowship promised me.
What friend were best me of to provide?   390
I lose my time here longer to abide.
Yet in my mind a thing there is:
All my life I have loved riches;
If that my Good now help me might,
He would make my heart full light.   395
I will speak to him in this distress.
Where art thou my Goods and riches?

GOODS (*From within*)   Who calleth me? Everyman? What! hast thou haste?
I lie here in corners, trussed and piled so high,
And in chests I am locked so fast,   400
Also sacked in bags—thou mayst see with thine eye—
I cannot stir; in packs low I lie.
What would ye have? Lightly* me say.

EVERYMAN   Come hither, Goods, in all the haste thou may.
For a counsel I must desire thee.   405

(*Enter* GOODS)

GOODS   Sir, and ye in the world have sorrow or adversity,
That can I help you to remedy shortly.

EVERYMAN   It is another disease that grieveth me;
In this world it is not, I tell thee so.   410
I am sent for another way to go,
To give a strait count general
Before the highest Jupiter of all;
And all my life I have had joy and pleasure in thee.
Therefore I pray thee go with me,   415
For, peradventure, thou mayst before God Almighty
My reckoning help to clean and purify;
For it is said ever among,
That "money maketh all right that is wrong."

384 Eager.
403 Quickly.

GOODS   Nay, Everyman; I sing another song,   420
    I follow no man in such voyages;
    For, and I went with thee,
    Thou shouldst fare much the worse for me;
    For because on me thou did set thy mind,
    Thy reckoning I have made blotted and blind,   425
    That thine account thou cannot make truly;
    And that hast thou for the love of me.

EVERYMAN   That would grieve me full sore,
    When I should come to that fearful answer.
    Up, let us go thither together.   430

GOODS   Nay, not so! I am too brittle, I may not endure;
    I will follow no man one foot, be ye sure.

EVERYMAN   Alas! I have thee loved, and had great pleasure
    All my life-days on goods and treasure.

GOODS   That is to thy damnation, without lesing!*   435
    For my love is contrary to the love everlasting.
    But if thou had me loved moderately during,
    As to the poor to give part of me,
    Then shouldst thou not in this dolor be,
    Nor in this great sorrow and care.   440

EVERYMAN   Lo, now was I deceived ere I was ware,
    And all I may wyte* my spending of time.

GOODS   What, weenest thou that I am thine?

EVERYMAN   I had weened so.

GOODS   Nay, Everyman, I say no;   445
    As for a while I was lent thee,
    A season thou hast had me in prosperity.
    My condition is man's soul to kill;
    If I save one, a thousand I do spill;
    Weenest thou that I will follow thee?   450
    Nay, not from this world, verily.

EVERYMAN   I had weened otherwise.

GOODS   Therefore to thy soul Goods is a thief;
    For when thou art dead, this is my guise—
    Another to deceive in the same wise   455
    As I have done thee, and all to his soul's reprief.

EVERYMAN   O false Goods, curséd thou be!
    Thou traitor to God, that hast deceived me
    And caught me in thy snare.

GOODS   Mary! thou brought thyself in care;   460
    Whereof I am right glad.
    I must needs laugh, I cannot be sad.

EVERYMAN   Ah, Goods, thou hast had long my hearty love;
    I gave thee that which should be the Lord's above.

435 Lying.
442 Blame to.

But wilt thou not go with me indeed?   465
    I pray thee truth to say.
GOODS   No, so God me speed!
    Therefore farewell, and have good day. (*Exit* GOODS)
EVERYMAN   O, to whom shall I make my moan
    For to go with me in that heavy journey?   470
    First Fellowship said he would with me gone;
    His words were very pleasant and gay,
    But afterward he left me alone.
    Then spake I to my kinsmen, all in despair,
    And also they gave me words fair,   475
    They lacked no fair speaking,
    But all forsook me in the ending.
    Then went I to my Goods, that I loved best,
    In hope to have comfort, but there had I least;
    For my Goods sharply did me tell   480
    That he bringeth many into hell.
    Then of my self I was ashamed,
    And so I am worthy to be blamed;
    Thus may I well my self hate.
    Of whom shall I now counsel take?   485
    I think that I shall never speed
    Till that I go to my Good Deeds.
    But alas! is so weak
    That she can neither go nor speak.
    Yet will I venture on her now.   490
    My Good Deeds, where be you?
            (GOOD DEEDS *speaks from the ground*)
GOOD DEEDS   Here I lie, cold in the ground.
    Thy sins hath me sore bound,
    That I cannot stir.   495
EVERYMAN   O Good Deeds! I stand in fear;
    I must you pray of counsel,
    For help now should come right well.
GOOD DEEDS   Everyman, I have understanding
    That ye be summoned account to make   500
    Before Messias, of Jerusalem King;
    And you do by me,* that journey with you will I take.
EVERYMAN   Therefore I come to you my moan to make;
    I pray you that ye will go with me.
GOOD DEEDS   I would full fain, but I cannot stand, verily.   505
EVERYMAN   Why, is there anything on you fall?
GOOD DEEDS   Yea, sir, I may thank you of all;
    If ye had perfectly cheered me,
    Your book of count full ready had be. (GOOD DEEDS *shows him the Book*)

---

502 That is, "If you will act by my advice."

Look, the books of your works and deeds eke;*   510
Ah, see how they lie under the feet,
To your soul's heaviness.
EVERYMAN   Our Lord Jesus, help me!
For one letter here I can not see.
GOOD DEEDS   There is a blind reckoning in time of distress!   515
EVERYMAN   Good Deeds, I pray you, help me in this need,
Or else I am for ever damned indeed;
Therefore help me to make my reckoning
Before the Redeemer of all thing,
That King is, and was, and ever shall.   520
GOOD DEEDS   Everyman, I am sorry of your fall,
And fain would I help you, and I were able.
EVERYMAN   Good Deeds, your counsel I pray you give me.
GOOD DEEDS   That shall I do verily;
Though that on my feet I may not go,   525
I have a sister that shall with you also,
Called Knowledge, which shall with you abide,
To help you to make that dreadful reckoning.
(*Enter* KNOWLEDGE)
KNOWLEDGE   Everyman, I will go with thee, and be thy guide,   530
In thy most need to go by thy side.
EVERYMAN   In good condition I am now in every thing,
And am wholly content with this good thing;
Thanked be God my Creator.
GOOD DEEDS   And when he hath brought thee there,   535
Where thou shalt heal thee of thy smart,
Then go you with your reckoning and your Good Deeds together
For to make you joyful at heart
Before the blesséd Trinity.
EVERYMAN   My Good Deeds, gramercy!   540
I am well content, certainly,
With your words sweet.
KNOWLEDGE   Now go we together lovingly
To Confession, that cleansing river.
EVERYMAN   For joy I weep; I would we were there!   545
But, I pray you, give me cognition
Where dwelleth that holy man, Confession.
KNOWLEDGE   In the house of salvation;
We shall find him in that place,
That shall us comfort, by God's grace.   550
(KNOWLEDGE *leads* EVERYMAN *to* CONFESSION)
Lo, this is Confession. Kneel down and ask mercy,
For he is in good conceit* with God almighty.

510 Also.
553 High esteem.

EVERYMAN (*Kneeling*)   O glorious fountain, that all uncleanness doth clarify,
Wash from me the spots of vice unclean, 555
That on me no sin may be seen.
I come, with Knowledge, for my redemption,
Redempt with hearty and full contrition;
For I am commanded a pilgrimage to take,
And great accounts before God to make. 560
Now, I pray you, Shrift, mother of salvation,
Help my Good Deeds for my piteous exclamation.
CONFESSION   I know your sorrow well, Everyman.
Because with Knowledge ye come to me,
I will you comfort as well as I can, 565
And a precious jewel I will give thee,
Called penance, voider of adversity;
Therewith shall your body chastised be,
With abstinence, and perseverance in God's service.
Here shall you receive that scourge of me, (*Gives* EVERYMAN *a scourge*) 570
Which is penance strong, that ye must endure
To remember thy Savior was scourged for thee
With sharp scourges, and suffered it patiently;
So must thou, or thou 'scape that painful pilgrimage.
Knowledge, keep him in this voyage, 575
And by that time Good Deeds will be with thee.
But in any wise be seeker of mercy,
For your time draweth fast, and ye will saved be;
Ask God mercy, and He will grant truly;
When with the scourge of penance man doth him bind, 580
The oil of forgiveness then shall he find. (*Exit* CONFESSION)
EVERYMAN   Thanked be God for his gracious work!
For now I will my penance begin;
This hath rejoiced and lighted my heart,
Though the knots be painful and hard within. 585
KNOWLEDGE   Everyman, look your penance that ye fulfil,
What pain that ever it to you be,
And Knowledge shall give you counsel at will
How your account ye shall make clearly.
(EVERYMAN *kneels*) 590
EVERYMAN   O eternal God! O heavenly figure!
O way of righteousness! O goodly vision!
Which descended down in a virgin pure
Because he would Everyman redeem,
Which Adam forfeited by his disobedience. 595
O blessèd Godhead! elect and high divine,
Forgive me my grievous offence;
Here I cry thee mercy in this presence.
O ghostly treasure! O ransomer and redeemer!
Of all the world hope and conductor, 600

Mirror of joy, and founder of mercy,
Which illumineth heaven and earth thereby,
Hear my clamorous complaint, though it late be.
Receive my prayers; unworthy of they benignity.
Though I be a sinner most abominable,   605
Yet let my name be written in Moses' table.
O Mary! pray to the Maker of all thing,
Me for to help at my ending,
And save me from the power of my enemy,
For Death assaileth me strongly.   610
And, Lady, that I may by means of thy prayer
Of your Son's glory to be partner,
By the means of his passion I it crave;
I beseech you, help my soul to save. (*He rises*)
Knowledge, give me the scourge of penance.   615
My flesh therewith shall give a quittance.
I will now begin, if God give me grace.
KNOWLEDGE   Everyman, God give you time and space.
Thus I bequeath you in the hands of our Savior,
Now may you make your reckoning sure.   620
EVERYMAN   In the name of the Holy Trinity,
My body sore punished shall be. (*Scourges himself*)
Take this, body, for the sin of the flesh;
Also thou delightest to go gay and fresh,
And in the way of damnation thou did me bring;   625
Therefore suffer now strokes of punishing.
Now of penance I will wade the water clear,
To save me from purgatory, that sharp fire. (GOOD DEEDS *rises from floor*)
GOOD DEEDS   I thank God, now I can walk and go,
And am delivered of my sickness and woe.   630
Therefore with Everyman I will go, and not spare;
His good works I will help him to declare.
KNOWLEDGE   Now, Everyman, be merry and glad;
Your Good Deeds cometh now; ye may not be sad;
Now is your Good Deeds whole and sound,   635
Going upright upon the ground.
EVERYMAN   My heart is light, and shall be evermore.
Now will I smite faster than I did before.
GOOD DEEDS   Everyman, pilgrim, my special friend,
Blesséd be thou without end;   640
For thee is prepared the eternal glory.
Ye have me made whole and sound,
Therefore I will bide by thee in every stound.*
EVERYMAN   Welcome, my Good Deeds; now I hear thy voice,
I weep for very sweetness of love.   645
KNOWLEDGE   Be no more sad, but ever rejoice;

643 At all times.

God seeth thy living in his throne above.
Put on this garment to thy behoof,*
Which is wet with your tears,
Or else before God you may it miss, 650
When you to your journey's end come shall.

EVERYMAN   Gentle Knowledge, what do ye it call?

KNOWLEDGE   It is the garment of sorrow;
From pain it will you borrow;
Contrition it is 655
That getteth forgiveness;
It pleaseth God passing well.

GOOD DEEDS   Everyman, will you wear it for your heal?

(EVERYMAN *puts on garment of contrition*)

EVERYMAN   Now blesséd be Jesu, Mary's Son! 660
For now have I on true contrition.
And let us go now without tarrying;
Good Deeds, have we clear our reckoning?

GOOD DEEDS   Yea, indeed I have it here.

EVERYMAN   Then I trust we need not fear. 665
Now, friends, let us not part in twain.

KNOWLEDGE   Nay, Everyman, that will we not, certain.

GOOD DEEDS   Yet must thou lead with thee
Three persons of great might.

EVERYMAN   Who should they be? 670

GOOD DEEDS   Discretion and Strength they hight,*
And thy Beauty may not abide behind.

KNOWLEDGE   Also ye must call to mind
Your Five Wits as for your counselors.

GOOD DEEDS   You must have them ready at all hours. 675

EVERYMAN   How shall I get them hither?

KNOWLEDGE   You must call them all together,
And they will hear you incontinent.*

EVERYMAN   My friends, come hither and be present;
Discretion, Strength, my Five Wits, and Beauty. 680

(*Enter* DISCRETION, STRENGTH, FIVE WITS, *and* BEAUTY)

BEAUTY   Here at your will we be all ready.
What will ye that we should do?

GOOD DEEDS   That ye would with Everyman go,
And help him in his pilgrimage. 685
Advise you, will ye with him or not in that voyage?

STRENGTH   We will bring him all thither,
To his help and comfort, ye may believe me.

DISCRETION   So will we go with him all together.

EVERYMAN   Almighty God, lovéd may thou be, 690

---

648 Benefit.
671 Are called.
678 Immediately.

162   ANONYMOUS

I give thee laud that I have hither brought
Strength, Discretion, Beauty, and Five Wits. Lack I naught;
And my Good Deeds, with Knowledge clear,
All be in company at my will here.
I desire no more to my business.   695
STRENGTH   And I, Strength, will by you stand in distress,
Through thou would in battle fight on the ground.
FIVE WITS   And though it were through the world round,
We will not depart for sweet nor sour.
BEAUTY   No more will I, unto death's hour,   700
Whatsoever thereof befall.
DISCRETION   Everyman, advise you first of all;
Go with a good advisement and deliberation.
We all give you virtuous monition*
That all shall be well.   705
EVERYMAN   My friends, hearken what I will tell:
I pray God reward you in his heavenly sphere.
Now hearken, all that be here,
For I will make my testament
Here before you all present: 710
In alms half my goods I will give with my hands twain
In the way of charity, with good intent,
And the other half still shall remain,
I it bequeath to be returned there it ought to be.
This I do in despite of the fiend of hell,   715
To go quite out of his peril
Ever after and this day.
KNOWLEDGE   Everyman, hearken what I say;
Go to Priesthood, I you advise,
And receive of him in any wise   720
The holy sacrament and ointment together;
Then shortly see ye turn again hither;
We will all abide you here.
FIVE WITS   Yea, Everyman, hie you that ye ready were.
There is no emperor, king, duke, nor baron,   725
That of God hath commission
As hath the least priest in the world being;
For of the blessèd sacraments pure and benign
He beareth the keys, and thereof hath the cure
For man's redemption—it is ever sure—   730
Which God for our soul's medicine
Gave us out of his heart with great pain,
Here in this transitory life, for thee and me.
The blessèd sacraments seven there be:
Baptism, confirmation, with priesthood good,   735
And the sacrament of God's precious flesh and blood,

704 Assurance.

Marriage, the holy extreme unction, and penance.
These seven be good to have in remembrance,
Gracious sacraments of high divinity.

EVERYMAN   Fain would I receive that holy body   740
And meekly to my ghostly father* I will go.

FIVE WITS   Everyman, that is the best that ye can do.
God will you to salvation bring,
For priesthood exceedeth all other thing;
To us Holy Scripture they do teach,   745
And converteth man from sin heaven to reach;
God hath to them more power given,
Than to any angel that is in heaven.
With five words he may consecrate
God's body in flesh and blood to make,   750
And handleth his Maker between his hands.
The priest bindeth and unbindeth all bands,
Both in earth and in heaven;
Thou ministers all the sacraments seven;
Though we kissed thy feet, thou wert worthy;   755
Thou art the surgeon that cureth sin deadly:
No remedy we find under God
But all only priesthood.
Everyman, God gave priests that dignity,
And setteth them in his stead among us to be;   760
Thus be they above angels in degree.

        (*Exit* EVERYMAN *to receive the last rites of the church*)

KNOWLEDGE   If priests be good, it is so, surely;
But when Jesus hanged on the cross with great smart,
There he gave out of his blesséd heart   765
The same sacrament in great torment.
He sold them not to us, that Lord omnipotent.
Therefore Saint Peter the Apostle doth say
That Jesus' curse hath all they
Which God their Savior do buy or sell;   770
Or they for any money do take or tell.
Sinful priests giveth the sinners example bad;
Their children sitteth by other men's fires, I have heard;
And some haunteth women's company
With unclean life, as lusts of lechery.   775
These be with sin made blind.

FIVE WITS   I trust to God no such may we find.
Therefore let us priesthood honor,
And follow their doctrine for our souls' succor.
We be their sheep, and they shepherds be   780
By whom we all be kept in surety.

[741] Spiritual father.

Peace! for yonder I see Everyman come,
Which hath made true satisfaction.

GOOD DEEDS   Methinketh it is he indeed.

                              785

(*Re-enter* EVERYMAN)

EVERYMAN   Now Jesu be your alder speed.*
I have received the sacrament for my redemption,
And then mine extreme unction.
Blesséd be all they that counseled me to take it!
And now, friends, let us go without longer respite.   790
I thank God that ye have tarried so long.
Now set each of you on this rod your hand,
And shortly follow me.
I go before, there I would be. God be our guide.

STRENGTH   Everyman, we will not from you go,   795
Till ye have gone this voyage long.

DISCRETION   I, Discretion, will bide by you also.

KNOWLEDGE   And though this pilgrimage be never so strong,
I will never part you fro.
Everyman, I will be as sure by thee   800
As ever I did by Judas Maccabee.* (*They proceed together to the grave*)

EVERYMAN   Alas! I am so faint I may not stand,
My limbs under me do fold.
Friends, let us not turn again to this land,
Not for all the world's gold;   805
For into this cave must I creep
And turn to earth, and there to sleep.

BEAUTY   What, into this grave? Alas!

EVERYMAN   Yea, there shall you consume, more and less.*

BEAUTY   And what! should I smother here?   810

EVERYMAN   Yea, by my faith, and never more appear.
In this world live no more we shall,
But in heaven before the highest Lord of all.

BEAUTY   I cross out all this; adieu, by Saint John;
I take my cap in my lap and am gone.   815

EVERYMAN   What, Beauty, whither will ye?

BEAUTY   Peace! I am deaf. I look not behind me,
Not and thou would give me all the gold in thy chest. (*Exit* BEAUTY)

EVERYMAN   Alas, whereto may I trust?
Beauty goeth fast away from me;   820
She promised with me to live and die.

STRENGTH   Everyman, I will thee also forsake and deny.
Thy game liketh me not at all.

---

786 That is, "Your best help."

801 Judas Maccabeus, a great Hebrew hero of the second century B.C., was wise and shrewd, as well as courageous.

809 Both important and unimportant persons.

EVERYMAN   Why, then ye will forsake me all!
    Sweet Strength, tarry a little space.   825
STRENGTH   Nay, sir, by the rood of grace,
    I will hie me from thee fast,
    Though thou weep till thy heart to-brast.*
EVERYMAN   Ye would ever bide by me, ye said.
STRENGTH   Yea, I have you far enough conveyed;   830
    Ye be old enough, I understand,
    Your pilgrimage to take on hand.
    I repent me that I hither came.
EVERYMAN   Strength, you to displease I am to blame;
    Will you break promise that is debt?   835
STRENGTH   In faith, I care not;
    Thou art but a fool to complain.
    You spend your speech and waste your brain;
    Go, thrust thee into the ground. (*Exit* STRENGTH)
EVERYMAN   I had weened surer I should you have found.   840
    He that trusteth in his Strength
    She him deceiveth at the length.
    Both Strength and Beauty forsaketh me,
    Yet they promised me fair and lovingly.
DISCRETION   Everyman, I will after Strength be gone;   845
    As for me I will leave you alone.
EVERYMAN   Why, Discretion! will ye forsake me?
DISCRETION   Yea, in faith, I will go from thee;
    For when Strength goeth before
    I follow after evermore.   850
EVERYMAN   Yet, I pray thee, for the love of the Trinity,
    Look in my grave once piteously.
DISCRETION   Nay, so nigh will I not come.
    Farewell, every one! (*Exit* DISCRETION)
EVERYMAN   O all thing faileth, save God alone;   855
    Beauty, Strength, and Discretion;
    For when Death bloweth his blast
    They all run from me full fast.
FIVE WITS   Everyman, my leave now of thee I take;
    I will follow the other, for here I thee forsake.   860
EVERYMAN   Alas! then may I wail and weep,
    For I took you for my best friend.
FIVE WITS   I will no longer thee keep;
    Now farewell, and there an end. (*Exit* FIVE WITS)
EVERYMAN   O Jesu, help! all hath forsaken me!   865
GOOD DEEDS   Nay, Everyman; I will bide with thee,
    I will not forsake thee indeed;
    Thou shalt find me a good friend at need.

    [828] Burst to bits.

EVERYMAN   Gramercy, Good Deeds! now may I true friends see; 870
 They have forsaken me, every one;
 I loved them better than my Good Deeds alone.
 Knowledge, will ye forsake me also?
KNOWLEDGE   Yea, Everyman, when ye to death shall go;
 But not yet, for no manner of danger.
EVERYMAN   Gramercy, Knowledge, with all my heart. 875
KNOWLEDGE   Nay, yet I will not from hence depart
 Till I see where ye shall be come.
EVERYMAN   Methink, alas, that I must be gone
 To make my reckoning and my debts pay,
 For I see my time is nigh spent away. 880
 Take example, all ye that this do hear or see,
 How they that I loved best do forsake me,
 Except my Good Deeds that bideth truly.
GOOD DEEDS   All earthly things is but vanity.
 Beauty, Strength, and Discretion do man forsake, 885
 Foolish friends and kinsmen, that fair spake,
 All fleeth save Good Deeds, and that am I.
EVERYMAN   Have mercy on me, God most mighty;
 And stand by me, thou Mother and Maid, holy Mary!
GOOD DEEDS   Fear not, I will speak for thee. 890
EVERYMAN   Here I cry God mercy!
GOOD DEEDS   Short our end, and minish our pain.
 Let us go and never come again.
EVERYMAN   Into thy hands, Lord, my soul I commend.
 Receive it, Lord, that it be not lost. 895
 As thou me boughtest, so me defend,
 And save me from the fiend's boast,
 That I may appear with that blesséd host
 That shall be saved at the day of doom.
 In manus tuas—of might's most 900
 For ever—*commendo spiritum meum.**
(EVERYMAN and GOOD DEEDS descend into the grave)
KNOWLEDGE   Now hath he suffered that we all shall endure;
 The Good Deeds shall make all sure.
 Now hath he made ending.
 Methinketh that I hear angels sing 905
 And make great joy and melody
 Where Everyman's soul received shall be.
ANGEL (*Within*)   Come, excellent elect spouse to Jesu.
 Here above thou shalt go 910
 Because of thy singular virtue.
 Now the soul is taken the body fro,
 Thy reckoning is crystal-clear.

<hr>

901 "Into thy hands . . . I commend my spirit."

Now shalt thou in to the heavenly sphere,
Unto the which all ye shall come   915
That liveth well before the day of doom. (*Exit* KNOWLEDGE)
                    (*Enter* DOCTOR *as Epilogue*)
DOCTOR   This moral men may have in mind;
    Ye hearers, take it of worth, old and young,
    And forsake pride, for he deceiveth you in the end,   920
    And remember Beauty, Five Wits, Strength, and Discretion,
    They all at the last do Everyman forsake,
    Save his Good Deeds there doth he take.
    But beware, and they be small
    Before God he hath no help at all.   925
    None excuse may be there for Everyman.
    Alas, how shall he do then?
    For, after death, amends may no man make,
    For then mercy and pity do him forsake.
    If his reckoning be not clear when he do come,   930
    God will say—*"ite, maledicti, in ignem æternum."**
    And he that hath his account whole and sound,
    High in heaven he shall be crowned.
    Unto which place God bring us all thither,
    That we may live body and soul together.   935
    Thereto help the Trinity,
    Amen, say ye, for Saint Charity.

            Thus endeth this moral play of Everyman.

                              2C2198